BENNETTS ASSOCIATES
FOUR COMMENTARIES

CONTENTS

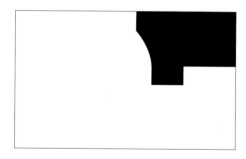

Museum of the Moving Image, London, p120
Client British Film Institute
Structural Engineer Waterman Partnership
Services Engineer The Kut Partnership
Exhibition Designer Land Design Studio
Access Consultant All Clear Design
Cost Consultant Davis Langdon & Everest

New Street Square, City of London, p122
Client Land Securities
Client Adviser Simon Harris & Co
Structural Engineer Pell Frischmann
Services Engineer Cundall Johnson
& Partners
Cladding Consultant Emmer Pfenninger
Fire Engineer Jeremy Gardner Associates
Landscape Architect Whitelaw Turkington
Public Art Consultant Modus Operandi
Lighting Consultant Speirs & Major
Acoustic Consultant Hann Tucker
Associates
Traffic Consultant Ove Arup
Sustainability Manager Element 4
Cost Consultant Davis Langdon
Planning Consultant DP9
Design-Build Contractor Sir Robert
McAlpine

Olympic Aquatics Centre Competition, London, p126
Client London 2012
Architect Bennetts Associates with
Studio Zoppini Associati
Structural and Services Engineer
Buro Happold
Landscape Architect Jenkins and Clarke
Public Art Consultant Modus Operandi
Events Facilities ESS
Cost Consultant Davis Langdon

Peel Park, Blackpool, p150
Client Land Securities Trillium
Landscape Architect Ian White Associates
Structural Engineer Buro Happold
Services Engineer Ernest Griffiths & Son
Cost Consultant Davis Langdon & Everest

PowerGen Headquarters, Coventry, p152
Client PowerGen plc
Structural Engineer Curtins
Consulting Engineers
Services Engineer Ernest Griffiths & Son
Landscape Architect Mark Westcott Design
Acoustic Consultant Arup Acoustics
Cost Consultant EC Harris
Project Manager Buro Four Project
Services
Design-Build Contractor Laing Midlands

Rail Traffic Control Centre (West Coast, Birmingham), p158
Client Network Rail (West Coast Route
Modernisation)
Lead Consultant and Engineer Parsons
Brinckerhoff Ltd
Cost Consultant EC Harris
Design-Build Contractor Birse
Construction Ltd

Rail Traffic Control Centre (Thameslink, London), p158
Client Thameslink 2000
Structural Engineer Jacobs Gibb
Services Engineer Jacobs Gibb
Cost Consultant Franklin & Andrews
Design-Build Contractor Morrison
Construction Ltd

Reading Office Development, Berkshire, p160
Client Speyhawk Land & Estates
Structural Engineer Franks & Lewin
Services Engineer Roger Cuthbert
Associates
Landscape Consultant Charles Funke
Associates
Cost Consultant Wheeler Group
Consultancy
Design Manager Buro Four Project services
Contractor Tellings Limited

The Richard Attenborough Centre for Disability and the Arts, Leicester University, p164
Client University of Leicester
Architect Ian Taylor with Bennetts
Associates
Structural Engineer Curtins Consulting
Engineers
Services Engineer David Beattie
Associates
Acoustic Consultant Arup Acoustics
Cost Consultant Michael Latham
Associates
Contractor Laing Midlands

The Royal College of Pathologists, London, p166
Client The Royal College of Pathologists
Structural Engineer Price & Myers (Phase
1), Alan Baxter & Associates (Phase 2)
Services Engineer David Beattie
Associates
Cost Consultant Michael Latham
Associates
Management Contractor Team
Management (Phase 1)

Sophos Headquarters, Abingdon, p170
Client Sophos plc
Structural Engineer Curtins Consulting
Engineers
Services Engineer Ernest Griffiths & Son
Landscape Architect Land Use Consultants
Cost Consultant Davis Langdon & Everest
Project Manager Atkins Faithful and Gould
Contractor Laing O'Rourke

University Departments, Potterrow, Edinburgh, p174
Client University of Edinburgh
Architect Bennetts Associates
with Reiach and Hall
Structural and Services Engineer
Buro Happold
Landscape Architect Ironside Farrar
Cost Consultant Turner Townsend Cost
Management

Waterloo Bus Station, London, p178
Client London Buses/Transport for London
Structural Engineer Benaim
Services Engineer W S Atkins
Cost Consultant Corderoy

Wessex Water Operations Centre, Bath, p180
Client Wessex Water
Client Representative Tim Hamilton
Associates
Structural Engineer and Services
Buro Happold
Landscape Architect Bernard Ede/
Grant Associates
Cost Consultant Davis Langdon & Everest
Project Manager Buro Four Project
Services
Construction Manager MACE
Art Consultant Modus Operandi
Sustainability Consultant BRE

BENNETTS ASSOCIATES

Nina Abel, Je Ahn, Doug Allard Helen Allen, Keith Andrews, Steven Anderson, Tim Anstey, Hannah Armitage, Vanessa Bartoluvic, Stephen Bates, Till Beier, Denise Bennetts, Rab Bennetts, Chloe Biggins, John Bloomfield, Ann Bodkin, Satya Bosman, Andrew Bowyer, Dan Burr, Jane Burridge, Jo Burtenshaw, Karen Cadell, Sebastian Camisuli, Michael Cant, Richard Castor Jeffery, Greg Chapman, Denise Chase, Elvin Chatergon, Edward Checkley, Paddi Clark, Richard Cohen, Carol Cottrell, Andrea Crumbach, Jason Curtis, Alison Darvill, Tobias Davidson, Pereen D'Avoine, Mark Dawson, Eugenie Denchfield, Ann-Marie Diderich, Nick Dodd, Simon Doody, Aimee Doyle, Paula Edwards, Ron Elkins, Richard Ellis, Christopher Enti, Ulrika Eriksson, Simon Erridge, Jerry Evans, Jonny Fisher, Peter Fisher, Martina Focchi, Kevin Galvin, Suzanne Garrod, Carolyn Gembles, Yvonne Gibbs, Alasdair Gordon, Alison Grieg, Anja Grossmann, Carina Hall, Tim Hall, Laurie Hallows, Samir Hamaiel, Hjortur Hannesson, Louise Hansen, Bjork Haraldsdottir, Wendy Harcus, John Harding, Sarah Hare, Jude Harris, Graham Haworth, David Head, Amanda Heal, David Henderson, Michael Holzrichter, Michelle Hood, Heike Hower, Anisa Hussein, David Jensen, Arthur Ka Ho Cheung, Jerome Keam, Ray Kearney, Chris Kelly, Robyn Kelly, Mike Kininmonth, Andy Kirk, Emiel Koole, Thomas Koppelman, David Laing, Leanne Lake, Jasmine Lamey, Nicole Lamperti,

Kia Larsdotter, Ulla Larsen, Susanna Laughton, Ute Leibe, Wing-Shun Leung, Julian Lipscombe, David Liston, Sam Lloyd, Marcus Lobmaier, Stefano Longhi, Rene Lotz, Jane Lowe, Kirsty Maguire, Chris Mascall, Jon Matthews, Stuart McBriar, Sarah McDougall, Steve McKay, Alasdair McKenzie, Lorraine McLeod, Stuart McLoughlin, Magnus Menzefricke, John Miller, Bryn Mor, Colin Muir, Michelle Mumby, Mandy Murray, Kelly Nash, James Nelmes, Ronnie Neylan, Krista Norman, Mike O'Carroll, David Olson, Brendan O'Neill, Sven Ostner, Alison Overend, Monika Paarmann, Roman Pardon, Michael Pawlyn, Robert Payne, Debra Penn, Alex Philip, Tamzin Pike, Suzanne Pitcher, Jacqueline Pitfield, Chris Pope, Gary Power, Steven Rankin, Duncan Reed, Jonathan Riddle, Jo Rippon, Christoph Rohr, Moray Royles, Peter Runacres, Alison Sampson, Duncan Sanby, Florian Scheible, Carly Scott, Sam Scott, Claire Sharp, Svinder Singh, Sidhu Sofie Skoug, John Southall, Katrin Steinhoff, Anat Stern, Elisabeth Stockinger, Kristian Stoltz, Sybille Stolze, Melanie Sutherland, Adrienne Taylor, Ian Taylor, Steve Tompkins, David Tordoff, Mark Tuff, Hugo Tugman, Sylvia Ullmayer, Kristin Utz, Sophie Vickers, Pranvera Vula, Tracey Walshe, Elly Ward, Scott Wardlaw, Richard Warwick, Polly Waterworth, Stuart Watson, Doric Wells, Mark Westcott, David Whitton, Duncan Woodburn, Karen Wygers, Paul Wygers, Tumpa Yasmine, Margaret Yescombe, Jeremy Young

FOREWORD

This book chronicles the work of an architectural practice, not an architect; a method, not a style; collaboration, not individualism.

Conventional wisdom, or at least most books about architects, suggests that architecture is a solitary pursuit, where buildings are created by an architect or, perhaps, a partnership of two. There is rarely much recognition of the team in the background although those actually generating the drawings are often the source of critically important ideas, let alone the actual production of the project. Cultural values seem to favour the individual to the extent that the face of the architect is as likely to appear on some magazine covers as the building itself.

The reality of architectural practice, certainly at Bennetts Associates, is that the combination of individuals is far more potent than anything that could be achieved by the elitist master and studio relationship. Experience is important, but the balance of knowledge with exploration, of technical ability with creativity and of dogged application with long-range perspective has greater relevance for the attainment of architecture at a consistently high level than the presumption of superhuman qualities in one leading architect.

Although the perception of Bennetts Associates is inevitably bound up with the name of its founders, this is a firm that has built its portfolio on shared ideas and the electricity that flows from collaboration rather than solitary endeavour. The primary purpose of this book is to record what can only be described as a collective achievement – a wide-ranging body of work by a group of like-minded architects who believe that they can achieve more together than separately.

The chemistry that facilitates such a flat hierarchy is clearly important, but it has taken some time to realise how different it is from some other practices. Enjoyment and humour is, consciously, part of the formula. There is a buzz in the Bennetts Associates office and an absence of the fear that seems evident in the ateliers of some architects. How else are talented people supposed to be creative? Self-criticism is invited from all quarters and, equally, ideas are not monopolised by the few. This is not the preserve of the prima-donna; the only status is that of good architectural judgement.

18 years after Bennetts Associates was established there is a sufficient body of work to identify a number of recurring strands – an architectural DNA for the practice as it were – that illustrate how collaboration is not merely the

assembly of ideas from different people but is something more cohesive. Central to this is the notion of architectural integrity – a clarity of organisation and space that makes the two inseparable – supported by a structural language that determines the play of light as much as it does the technological solutions to many of the buildings.

The book, then, also presents the opportunity or, possibly, the obligation to restate these key precepts for consumption internally and externally alike and to consolidate the practice's 'manifesto'. It also charts how ideas have evolved, from the unfettered, laboratory conditions of the out-of-town business park to the complex responses required of cultural buildings in urban settings. Furthermore, the determination to avoid specialisation and remain a general architectural practice should be self-evident, with railway projects interspersed with education buildings, offices, a theatre and a concert venue, housing, urban regeneration and masterplanning, visitor centres, a public library and a sprinkling of competitions.

The glue that holds so many creative individuals and projects together is the practice's design method. Based on a rigorous analysis that always precedes design, this process is of necessity inclusive as it requires parallel investigation of all the project's constituent parts before workable solutions or architectural forms emerge.

In consequence, architecture based on style alone would not survive. Far from being emasculated by this process, the architect's authority is actually reinforced by a demonstrable understanding of the project's underlying nature and his or her ability to embrace the round-table contributions of other participants such as engineers, contractors and, of course, the client.

The attitudes that support this methodology seem wholly appropriate to current architectural practice in the UK, with its lingering perception that architects in this country may be among the most creative in the world but they lack the competence to deliver their ideas. For instance, Bennetts Associates' objective pursuit of sustainability and the proper conduct of construction exemplify a broad outlook that explains why much work emanates from project managers, engineers and contractors as well as direct from clients. Professionalism in implementation is not in any way seen as contradictory with the more formal qualities of Bennetts Associates' architecture which, ultimately, is

driven by deeply-held convictions that make the spaces and forms what they are.

To describe this approach to architecture in some depth, the four essays in this book deal in different ways with the values that drive it and the often neglected perceptions of those who experience it. The authors comprise two writer/ academics who are evaluating the practice for the first time and two consultants who have crossed professional paths with Bennetts Associates on a number of occasions.

Richard Weston teaches at Cardiff University and writes extensively about architecture. Here, he writes about construction and form from an historical perspective and the importance of holistic solutions to the firm's buildings. Francis Duffy – researcher, theorist and practitioner – deals with the design process, extending detailed consideration of one building type to the wider output of the practice. Art consultant Vivien Lovell examines collaboration through the medium of public art and describes the mood and feel of the buildings she has visited. Finally, former journal editor and head of the Cambridge School of Architecture Peter Carolin identifies from personal experience recurring qualities that embody the spirit of Bennetts Associates' work.

If the four commentaries provide expert opinion, the illustrated descriptions of 32 projects should allow readers to form their own. Interspersed in alphabetical groups between the essays, the evolution of ideas across a diverse range of work can be traced through completed buildings to work currently at the formative stages. The book concludes by recording the many people from Bennetts Associates and the other organisations who have underpinned the design process over the firm's first 18 years.

Although Bennetts Associates' projects have often been recognised through awards and building-studies in journals, this is the first book about Bennetts Associates. Its publication coincides with a major exhibition at the Royal Institute of British Architects in London.

RICHARD WESTON
CONSTRUCTION, STRUCTURE AND FORM

The connection between construction, structure and form is fundamental to much of Bennetts Associates' work and the degree to which it is explicit in the firm's architecture is explored by Richard Weston in this book's first commentary. Weston observes that the roots of this approach lie in mainstream early Modernism, but the manner of its development in North America and its subsequent interrogation by Louis Kahn led Bennetts Associates to pursue an altogether richer and more humane relationship between space and enclosure than seemed likely in the architectural climate that prevailed when the practice was formed in the late 1980s. Critical to this was the empirical logic of environmental engineering, which supported the spatial concerns of the firm's formative buildings. As the portfolio has evolved from innovative commercial developments to major public buildings, Weston applauds the almost obsessive application of construction and structural techniques in the pursuit of architectural integrity.

**Offices at
Devonshire Square**
Left: The loadbearing
steel facade

**Eugène-Emmanuel
Viollet-le-Duc**
Right: A project illustrating
the contrasting qualities
of cast iron and masonry

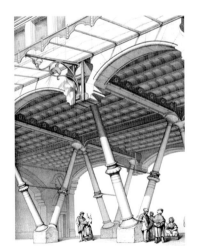

At first sight, Bennetts Associates' addition to Devonshire Square appears of a piece with the constructional vernacular of the new generation of buildings in the City of London: steel-framed for speed of construction; hugging the site boundaries to maximise its deep-plan floor areas; heavily glazed to make the most of available daylight. Look more closely, however, and you realise that it differs radically from almost everything around it. And what makes it different is plain to see but difficult to recognise, accustomed as we are to the idea that steel frames must be encased to protect them from fire, and insulated to avoid energy-sapping thermal bridges.

At Devonshire Square, however, the steelwork we see – robust, straight-as-a-die universal columns and beams – *is* the bearing structure of the building. We will return to explore briefly how this was achieved technically, but the more interesting immediate question is why the Bennetts team considered it worth the required effort in the first place. And to answer that, we must situate their work in the many-braided tradition of Modern architecture.

Finding appropriate expressions for multi-storey framed buildings was one of the major tasks faced by the first generation of manifestly 'Modern' architects more than a century ago. Materials new to large-scale building – cast and wrought iron, large sheets of glass and, later steel and the genuinely new reinforced concrete – challenged the foundations of Classicism, whose forms and aesthetic ideals were predicated upon conceiving of buildings as a solid 'body' of stone.

For the great French theorist Eugène-Emmanuel Viollet-le-Duc, the way ahead lay in a choice between the constructional clarity of Greek and Gothic architecture, and the deceits of Roman work, which he compared to "a man clothed: there is the man, and there is the dress; the dress may be good or bad, rich or poor in material, well or ill cut, but it forms no part of the body". In Gothic work, on the other hand, body and dress were inseparable: "supple, free, and as inquiring as the modern spirit: its principles permit the use of all the materials given by nature or industry". For Viollet, "constructive processes" were the proper basis of architectural form, which he argued would emerge effortlessly by using materials "according to their qualities and properties".

A potent demonstration of the structural rationalism espoused by Viollet-le-Duc came with the work of the first Chicago School – a touchstone for many in Bennetts Associates – and it was in designs such as William Le Baron Jenney's Leiter Building of 1889 that multi-storey skeletal construction first found clear architectural expression. Five years later, with the completion of the Chicago School's exquisite swansong, Burnham and Root's Reliance Building, a radical alternative was on offer. In place of the reassuring solidity of the Leiter Building, with its subdivision into large squares by clearly expressed column lines and floorplates, Burnham and Root offered continuous ribbons of reflective plate glass windows, alternating with narrower bands of glazed white tiles: the Classical body of stone had been transformed into a shimmering shaft of light.

The ideal of constructional discipline proclaimed with such clarity by Viollet-le-Duc and demonstrated by the architects of the Chicago School was to ripple through twentieth century architectural thought

and practice. In Mies van der Rohe's celebrated 1923 project for a glass skyscraper, the structural frame was set inside the building perimeter, and the envelope envisaged as an all-glass curtain hung from the top storey, by turns reflective and, Mies hoped, transparent – to reveal the skeleton within. The spatial freedom implicit in the distinction between structure and enclosure was, of course, the basis of the Modern 'free plan', of which Mies' Barcelona Pavilion of 1929 remains the purest model. But when he came to build his first tower, the Promontory Apartments of 1949, he opted to make the reinforced concrete frame the basis of the external expression.

For the steel framed apartments at 860–880 Lake Shore Drive in Chicago, completed two years later, Mies again rejected the divorce of structure and skin. Although fire protection meant that he could not show the actual structure, he represented it by means of structurally redundant I-sections that rhymed with, but were slightly larger than, the glazing mullions. It was pure artifice, a lie to tell the constructional truth, but by fusing structure and cladding in this way, Mies could hold on to the belief that the way a building looks should derive from the way it is made. With Lever House in New York, completed in 1953, Skidmore Owings and Merrill (SOM) reverted to the model of Mies' 1923 project – and of the Reliance Building. Setting the columns back from the facade, they enveloped the building in a uniform skin of steel and glass – precisely the kind of 'curtain wall' proposed by Mies 30 years before.

Lever House's offspring were destined to proliferate worldwide, and for as long as their curtain walls remained orthogonal assemblies of glass and spandrel panels, such buildings could be seen as exemplarily Modern expressions of the building technology of their time. But by effectively breaking the tie between the envelope and the underlying structure, the path had been opened both to the formal promiscuity of stylistic postmodernism and to an exploitation of the even more radical rift between surface and structure that came with the advent of rainscreen cladding.

In parallel with architectural approaches that exploited the disjunction between structure and form, speculative office development demanded a separation between the essential 'shell and core' (the domain of architect and engineer), and the 'fit-out' to meet a particular tenant's needs (as often as not the work of interior designers). The disturbing implications of these developments were perfectly summed up for Rab Bennetts when he interviewed the American architect Kevin Roche during a 1982 visit to his office in New Haven, Connecticut: steel construction in the USA, Roche warned him, is "reducing architecture to the wrapping on a candy bar".

The first major architect to be deeply troubled by the radical divorce between structure and form, and a central influence on the work of the Bennetts office, was Louis Kahn. For Kahn, materials, structure and space were inseparable. Spaces and forms made of brick and concrete should have fundamentally different qualities, and in place of the continuous universal, flowing space of orthodox Modernism, Kahn thought of a building's plan as a 'society of rooms' suited to different needs. Hence, for example, he formed the Kimbell Museum from a succession of concrete vaults that enable the interior to be experienced as both a continuous gallery floor and a succession of linear, room-like volumes. And contrary to the orthodox Modernist

PowerGen Headquarters
Left: The building is located on the outskirts of Coventry

Below: Typical floor plan, with coffered structure dotted

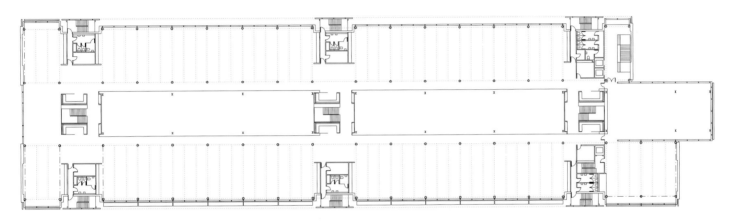

principle of separating buildings into mono-functional systems – structure, envelope, services, etc. – the structure was also, as Kahn put it, "the maker of light". This determination to address architectural problems holistically, to find forms that integrate functions and simultaneously defy gravity, shape space and control the environment, is central to the work of Bennetts Associates. It first found compelling expression in what has been described as "the most influential office building of the 1990s", the PowerGen Headquarters in Coventry.

PowerGen, one of two major UK providers of electricity, wanted a building that was both energy efficient and avoided the problems of Sick Building Syndrome associated with air-conditioned environments. Through developing their solution Bennetts came to question many of the orthodoxies of the 1980s. At 12 metres, the floorplate is relatively narrow – to facilitate natural ventilation and lighting – and the major circulation route is peripheral, rather than central, to avoid fragmenting the predominantly open plan offices. In place of the familiar horizontal flow of characterless space between raised floor and suspended ceiling, space is modulated by waves of shallow, subtly profiled concrete 'vaults'. Technically, they are recessed bays in a coffered slab, but spatially they feel like vaults, and the work they do is both structural and environmental, because by absorbing heat they become integral to the cooling and ventilation strategy.

The structural logic of the concrete slabs, deepening longitudinally towards the centre, thinning laterally between the ribs, is easily read – and rendered all the more satisfying by being applied both across the major spans and within each coffered bay. The result recalls, albeit in less muscular form (as befits the building's use), the

mighty slab that Jørn Utzon and Ove Arup conceived to support the public concourses at Sydney Opera House. In both, the forms are invitingly organic and bone-like, but whereas Utzon's design was determined by purely structural considerations, at PowerGen the final form also had to address planning and environmental factors.

The ribs are at 2.4 metre centres, as required by the 1.2 metre office planning grid, and to eliminate focussing of sound, the cross-section of the coffers is elliptical rather than circular. They are also designed to receive a continuous 'light raft' that both illuminates the offices and provides background lighting to the structure. The upward taper of the slab towards the open air on one side, and atrium on the other, recognises the forces at work – glossed over by the uniform, out-of-sight rectangular sections deployed in most such buildings – and helps to maximise the penetration of daylight.

Spatially, the succession of coffers echoes the spirit of Kahn's modulation of continuous space by vaulted rooms at the Kimbell Museum. But the finer scale of the predominantly open plan offices means that the effect is more like an intricate spatial fabric, the warp and weft of ribs and coffers lending architectural character to interiors that are generally, in the world of shell and core, relegated to the domain of interior design. Practically, the floor-to-structure heights were made sufficiently high to accept suspended ceilings, but architecturally their introduction would be an enormous loss.

The planning of PowerGen is also Kahnian in spirit, giving clear expression to the distinction between 'served' and 'servant' spaces. The linear atrium is subdivided by timber-clad 'service' towers: reached by narrow bridges, these contain stairs, coffee points and

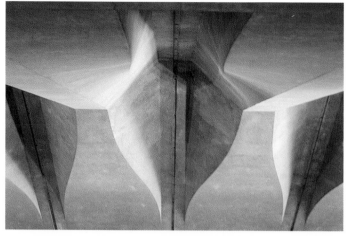

business centres, providing sociable meeting places at each office level. Non-standard spaces are pulled out beyond the office floorplates – main entrance, conference rooms and restaurant at one end; and the 'boiler room' of facilities reception, computer suite and the energy management centre for the power stations at the other.

The concrete structure at PowerGen was, as one might guess from its forms, cast in situ throughout, using GRP moulds. This permitted more compact beam sizes than would have been possible with precast members, and ensured that the joints in the slabs along the length of the offices could be kept absolutely straight. The structural continuity required by reinforced concrete also demanded that – unlike in the later, steel-framed building in Devonshire Square – the columns either be kept inside the cladding or, as at ground level, be fully exposed. The cladding chosen for the office floors consists of continuous bands of glazing, shaded by external louvres, and solid panels faced with stack-bonded bricks. To ensure that they did not appear load-bearing, the panels were post-tensioned by passing reinforcing rods through pre-formed holes in the engineering bricks, thereby enabling the contractor to build them under cover and hoist them into position.

The resulting expression feels almost industrial, and the dominant horizontality is punctuated, slightly uneasily to my eyes, by the enclosures of the fire escape stairs – Kahnian in their expression as 'servant' towers, but appearing slightly diffident to act as effective vertical counterpoints to the horizontal expression of the *fenêtres en longueur*. No such hesitations attend PowerGen's successor, the headquarters for John Menzies.

Completed in 1995, a year after its precursor, on Edinburgh's new business park masterplanned by Richard Meier, the John Menzies building deploys essentially the same strategy as that developed for PowerGen. The 12-metre office bays are arranged in a continuous U around a focal atrium, in response to the first of several linear water bodies – 'lochans' as they are called locally – created by the landscape architects, Ian White Associates. A transparent, fully-glazed block of meeting rooms and restaurant facilities occupies the front of the atrium and projects slightly beyond the 'official' building line: happily, this privileged space is communal, part of a continuous circulation loop around the atrium and allowing extensive views out.

The building's smaller size and compact plan eliminated the need for the internal staircase towers used at PowerGen, enabling the secondary stairs to double as fire escapes and leaving the building's perimeter free to be developed as a continuous curtain wall. In the project's early stages, reflecting Bennetts' love of expressed construction, the frame was to have been articulated on the facade. What emerged from the design development was an alternation of double-glazed panels containing non-retractable tilt-and-turn microblinds, and spandrels of toughened glass fritted with horizontal bands of white ceramic that cast mysterious shadows on the aluminium back-panels – hinting, like the microblinds, at unexpected layers within a physically shallow depth. At the corners, marking the presence of the stair and service cores, glass is replaced by a rainscreen of pale green, flame textured granite panels.

Seen on drawings, the Menzies facades might appear bland and uneventful, but in reality they create a calm, almost rhythmless

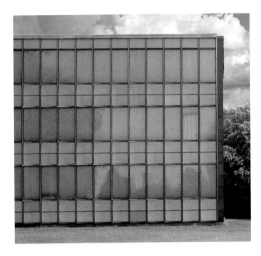

PowerGen Headquarters
Far left: Concrete ribs are
at 2.4 metre centres

Below left: The in situ
concrete under
construction

Jørn Utzon
Above left: Concrete
ribs to the Sydney Opera
House concourse, 1957

**John Menzies
Headquarters,
Edinburgh Park**
Below: Floor plan with
coffered structure dotted

Below right: General view
before construction of
neighbouring buildings

Arne Jacobsen
Above right: Rødovre
Town Hall, Denmark, 1955

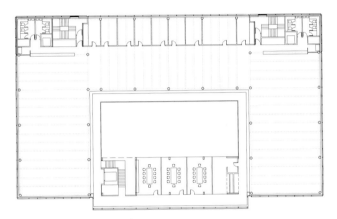

expression ideally suited to the gentle light and low sun of the north.
Is it merely coincidence, therefore, that in its use of different kinds
of glass and network-like character it brings to mind the work of Mies
van der Rohe's most refined European disciple, Arne Jacobsen? Not
the overtly Miesian Jacobsen so familiar in Britain, courtesy of St
Catherine's College, Oxford, but the earlier, more radical, designer of
Rødovre Town Hall in Denmark, where – as in the Menzies building
– a lingering Classical centrality of plan is set in tension with the
potentially infinite extension of the neutral, gridded facades that
play so artfully with the Danish light.

Structurally, the Menzies building differs significantly from
PowerGen in one major respect: the 12-metre wide coffered slabs
were manufactured off site in steel moulds. The design team originally
envisaged a wholly in situ structure, but during discussions with the
contractor it became clear that work could be speeded up by
developing a hybrid form in which the 40-centimetre diameter columns
were cast in situ prior to the arrival of the precast slab units – each
of which weighed 11 tonnes. The slabs were then set in position on
temporary supports while the perimeter ring beam and topping were
cast in one operation to tie all the elements together to form a
monolithic whole.

Architecturally, the principal consequence of the change from
in situ to precast construction was a somewhat increased depth and
bulk in the slab. This led to the decision to eliminate the curved, bow-
like ends and upward taper that were such a distinctive feature of the
coffers at PowerGen. At Menzies, the 'vaults' are of uniform section
and run neatly into the perimeter downstand beams, their undersides
set a few millimetres above the beams' soffits. These changes are
both logical and, in the broad sweep of architectural decisions, minor
– but not without their consequences.

At PowerGen the slabs appear to soar and float, and to invite
the offices to flow into the atrium; at Menzies the spaces feel more
contained, the structure more compartmented. Each is a logical,
unforced working out of constructional opportunities and constraints,
and each raises the quality of the workplace through the very means
– expressed structure – that so many designers of office buildings
have long assumed can no longer be used to shape and give
character to such spaces.

Bennetts Associates' second building on the new Edinburgh
Park, Alexander Graham Bell House for British Telecom (BT),
presented a schedule of accommodation both substantially larger
and more varied than that required by John Menzies, enabling them
to push further themes explored in each of the previous designs. In
essence, the plan consists of three slices of the arrangement adopted
at PowerGen, with offices – slightly deeper at 13.5 metres – flanking
a narrow, linear atrium. But here, three semi-autonomous such units
are ranged beside two wider, top-lit atria, one of which acts as the
entrance and reception area, the other as a garden court, replete
with trees, shrubs, timber decking, and channels of water and river-
washed pebbles.

BT's demand for an assortment of communal rooms – from
familiar meeting spaces to the 'break out' and 'touchdown' areas
demanded by modern working styles – enabled the plan to approach,
as Bennetts suggested in his account of the project published in

BT Edinburgh Park
Left: Internal volumes and
structures are visible from
the outside at night

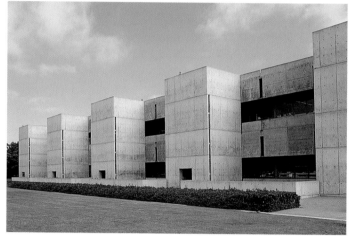

BT Edinburgh Park
Left: One of the stair
towers

Louis Kahn
Below: Stair towers
at the Salk Institute
for Biological Studies,
La Jolla, California, 1965

**Wessex Water
Operations Centre**
Right: *Brise-soleil* on
the south elevation

The Architects' Journal, the Kahnian ideal of a "society of rooms". Kahnian, too, is the handling of the stair and service cores as freestanding towers – the external elevations of the Salk Institute come to mind – and the decision to project a red cube containing the cafe, meeting rooms and executive offices into the adjacent lochan, and then to envelop it in a detached circular sunshade. The latter's materials – exposed steel and aluminium composite columns, and perforated aluminium solar shading blades – may border on high-tech, but the architectural lineage surely goes back to those circular concrete "ruins wrapped around buildings" which Kahn first essayed as solar protection in the unbuilt project for the Salk Meeting House.

Structurally, Bennetts reverted to in situ concrete, and the longitudinal tapers and asymmetry of the slabs duly reappeared. As at PowerGen, these refinements assist the penetration of light and movement of air and, thanks to the narrowness of the office atria, help to unite the spaces either side into a single social and working unit. The cladding, by contrast, pushed further the neutrality explored with the Menzies building. On the 'front' elevation to the lochan, the offices unfold behind a line of trees in a grid of uniformly-sized glass panels, a quiet foil to the projecting cube and circle, where the altogether more complex and playful games with form and light effectively command a major entrance to the Park.

Corporate office buildings rarely admit of major architectural innovations: God, as Mies believed of architecture *tout court*, is in the details. And Bennetts' details are quietly revealing of a determination to enrich the experiential qualities of the space. Take the balustrades to the office atria, for example. Building regulations, the pleasures of

spatial continuity, and the influx of natural light combine to demand glass. The orthodox solution would have the suitably toughened planes of glass disappear into the floor and be fixed back to the structure out of sight, with their tops capped by neat stainless steel tubes. Here, by contrast, the glass is visibly bolted back to the floor plate, and as the potential loads demand bolts at close centres, the result offers a visual satisfaction reminiscent of riveted steelwork. If this might appear slightly 'industrial', the handrail, in total contrast, is of warm, inviting hardwood, not cold steel. Each solution is entirely apt, if unexpected, and their combination adds richness to an interior of calm assurance. The full architectural and environmental potential of the ideas explored in the headquarters for PowerGen, Menzies and BT were conclusively demonstrated with the completion of the Wessex Water Operations Centre on the edge of Bath. Both the client, with their strong corporate commitment to sustainability, and the site were tailor-made for the Bennetts team's skills.

The steeply sloping land was generous in area and enjoyed stunning views over Salisbury Plain to the south, while to the north the new building would have to relate to a group of existing houses. The site's irregular shape and stone boundary wall also called for a more flexible response than the flatlands typical of the previous business parks, where the organisational diagram could be translated more or less directly into architectural form. Here, the accommodation is organised into three wings of two-storey, naturally ventilated offices, framing open-ended courtyards and stepping down a storey from wing to wing. An airy, top-lit internal 'street' links the offices, provides break out spaces, and ties in pavilions of stone-clad communal rooms

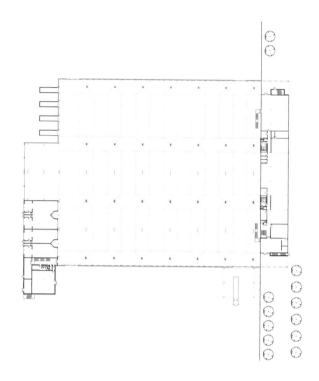

to the west, facing the best views.

Structurally, the design is a direct development from the earlier projects, but with two noticeable differences. The low-rise form allowed a frame of slender steel sections rather than in situ concrete, and the now familiar precast floor units are wider than before and, at a mere 65 millimetres thick, notably lighter. They are still sufficient in mass to provide the requisite passive cooling, but by using 50 per cent less material offer invaluable gains in sustainability terms, concrete not being a notably 'green' material. The results of these changes are dramatic. The entire fabric appear conspicuously lighter and airier, and the character of the architecture is shifted away from the gravitas of Kahn or Mies towards something more reminiscent of the 'kit of parts' aesthetic of Charles and Ray Eames.

Both the south and north facing office elevations are similarly glazed to ensure no diminution in the quality of light internally. To the south they are protected by fixed sunshades, whilst to the north, trees filter – and prevent unwanted heat gains from – the low angle late afternoon sun. This might appear to fly in the face of orthodox thinking about minimising north-facing glazing, but the Bennetts office's well known concern for sustainability is never allowed dogmatically to overwhelm the essential experiential quality of the places they create. The commitment to sustainability at Wessex Water was total, embracing everything from rainwater recycling to local sourcing of materials, biodiversity to detailed evaluations of operational and embedded energy. The result was the highest ever BREEAM (Building Research Establishment Energy Assessment Method) rating for a commercial office building and a predictable string of architectural awards.

Offices, both speculative and corporate, were the mainstay of many British practices during the 1980s and 90s, and it seems an apt barometer of the shift away from manufacturing in the UK during the 1990s that Bennetts' Associates first opportunity to build for seriously heavy industry should have come from a US-based company. And it was not just any company, but the Power Generation division of one of the most celebrated industrial patrons of modern architecture, the Cummins Engine Company, whose earlier UK facilities include the seminal Corten steel structured plant in Darlington by one of Rab Bennetts' American heroes, Roche Dinkeloo. This commission, for a diesel generator manufacturing facility on a still rural swathe of northwest Kent, was on a similarly monumental scale – and had to be complete in a mere 11 months.

Although built in steel rather than concrete, the Cummins factory has more in common with one of the now-demolished icons of post war industrial architecture, the Bryn Mawr Rubber Factory, than with the crop of high-tech factories and warehouses that for many constituted the most marketable recent face of British architecture. The difference has nothing to do with the choice of materials and everything to do with the architectural approach.

Just as Bennetts Associates is always determined to invest office buildings with the traditional architectural qualities of space, light and structure, so for Cummins it rejected any dalliance with the high-tech trappings of cables, masts and exposed mechanical services – all, so often, deployed largely for external image making rather than internal space making. The factory is conceived spatially, as a structure of top-lit vaults supported by a grid of truly monumental cruciform

Hampstead Theatre
Above: The foyer and bar

**Loch Lomond
Gateway and
Orientation Centre**
Right: Part of the 100
metre long oak colonnade

steel columns set 28 x 14 metres apart. The column shafts branch into four cantilever arms that define the zones of a tartan plan, and the primary bays are spanned by gently arched beams, with continuous bands of glazing at their crowns to bathe the interior in natural light. The accepted – 'natural' in a double sense – metaphor for such a space is 'forest of steel trees', but here the vast scale, regularity and visual presence of the structure recalls also the forest's most ancient architectural transformation, the hypostyle hall.

If clarity in marshalling space and structure to serve the client's operations is a hallmark of the Cummins design, it is equally apparent in far smaller and less process-driven projects such as the visitor centres designed for Heathrow Airport and Loch Lomond – the latter officially a 'Gateway and Orientation Centre'. The *parti* at Heathrow could hardly be simpler: two steel-framed 'thick walls' shelter the north and south facades, and support an inverted, curved roof – entirely rational in profile, structurally, but also nodding to the forms of aircraft wings.

To the north, the wall is largely solid and intended to be covered with climbing plants; to the south it is clad in two layers of frameless glazing to reduce sound and house solar control devices, escape stairs and cleaning equipment, while still allowing visitors more or less unrestricted views across to the runways. Extending beyond the enclosed spaces, and visually almost freestanding, the gridded steel walls seem to nod as much to the repetitive structures of Minimalist sculptures as to that now familiar Kahnian idea of the "wrapped ruin".

A Minimalist spirit also infuses the Loch Lomond facility, where the architecture is conceived as a calm frame for the splendours of the natural setting – which is, after all, the primary object of any visit for all but the occasional architectural tourist. A linear steel and glass pavilion houses the visitor facilities, and its relationship to the nearby, more commercial elements of the development is mediated by a 100-metre long timber colonnade. This is formed of large, evenly spaced timber sections which, thanks to the use of continuous steel sole and head plates that barely register visually, appear almost to float in space. Inside, the notoriously unruly exhibition design of such facilities is confined to a series of cubes set well back from the fully glazed perimeter, and these in turn are echoed by the cubic entrance volume and a glass-fronted box that breaks through the timber colonnade. To reinforce the link to the landscape, the end bay of the structure is free of glass, and cantilevered out over the adjacent water.

To my eyes, these smaller projects not only confirm the Bennetts office's commitment to grounding architectural form in a clear expression of structure and construction – in the 'making' of the buildings – but also suggest a slight but recognisable shift, or expansion, in the formal repertoire. This is confirmed by the two major cultural projects they have recently completed, the Hampstead Theatre in north London and the Central Library in Brighton.

In the theatre, the clarity of organisation is all we have come to expect, but both the treatment of the exterior – with its slightly fashionable random scatter of narrow glazed slots – and the rendering of the theatre as a zinc-clad space invader perched on jauntily angled legs, involved the exercise of architectural muscles that can easily atrophy on more constrained, commercial projects. The hint of playfulness is entirely apt to the commission, as is the surprising and

invitingly rich palette of materials deployed in the public spaces.

If the Hampstead Theatre confirms that the practice can operate inventively and convincingly outside the familiar box of repetitive, gridded space, the Brighton Central Library similarly illustrates how the spatial, environmental and structural repertoire developed in the commercial and industrial work can be deployed to address the challenge of a more complex programme. The library and adjoining cafe pavilion are at the heart of a 1.75-hectare redevelopment in the city's North Laine, framing two sides of a new square. The library itself is conceived as an extension of this space, with a three-storey U of support spaces wrapped around the two-storey reference library which, visually, opens onto the square through a fully-glazed, solar-shaded south elevation. The secondary spaces are almost domestic in scale, and overlook the library through large openings in a thick wall, which is bathed in natural light courtesy of a glazed slot between the central library and the perimeter accommodation. The arrangement evokes thoughts of a terrace of houses surrounding a small square, child-like in its distortion of scale and held in check from any too literal reading by the abstraction of the smooth, timber-clad surface of the framing wall.

The two-storey central volume, by contrast, is grandly structured by eight concrete 'trees', solidified miniatures, as it were, of the Cummins factory's steelwork that inevitably also bring to mind Frank Lloyd Wright's Johnson Wax Building. As in the latter, light spills between the structures, filtering down through upward migrating air that is drawn aloft by tall, sculptural wind towers that form a striking addition to Brighton's already exotic skyline. Externally, in addition to glass, the building is clad with rectangular ceramic tiles, a

reinterpretation of the 'mathematical tiles' familiar on some of the city's older buildings. Their variegation of colour and sheen is beguiling, connecting the building unmistakably to the burgeoning interest in architectural surfaces epitomised by the so-called 'Swiss Box' school of designers.

And so, finally, we return to where we began, to the exposed steel structure of Devonshire Square, which we can now understand as a product of that commitment to the expressive craft of building that lies at the core of the office's expertise. Unlike the other office buildings we have explored, Devonshire Square was a speculative development, and Bennetts' involvement was therefore confined to the 'shell and core', precluding the exposed concrete floor structures used in other projects. Any expression of structural 'truth' therefore had to be confined to the facade, with numerous attendant technical difficulties.

Cold bridging, the bane of attempts to expose structure externally courtesy of modern insulation requirements, was prevented by introducing a pad of insulating material between the end plates to create a thermal break, the alignment of which necessitated the welding of stub connections into the flanges of the facade beams to receive the secondary steel floor beams. Condensation within the structure was addressed by introducing insulation and a vapour barrier behind the facade beams, and to cope with weathering and physical deterioration, a special system of coatings was devised to give a design life of 20 years, by when major refurbishment could be expected. Finally, although steel is produced under factory conditions, quality control is concerned primarily with ensuring consistency of structural performance rather than uniformity of visual appearance.

Jørn Utzon
Far left:
Bagsærd Church, near
Copenhagen, Denmark,
1976

**Offices at
Devonshire Square**
Left: Interior/exterior
junction

Right: The steel structure
in the setting of a
conservation area

The contractor therefore had to select sections individually to ensure that they were straight and free of surface defects.

Faced with such complications, many might conclude that exposing a multi-storey steel structure borders on the obsessive. And so it does – but it is from this and similar obsessions that fine architecture emerges. The building is, naturally, painted in authentic Miesian colours, a cipher of architectural seriousness at one with the City's pinstripe suits, and as such differs radically from SOM's altogether less sober flaunting of steel structure at Ludgate Circus and Exchange House – just as it differs, albeit less conspicuously, from its curtain-walled, rainscreened and slick-skinned neighbours.

While visiting the Devonshire Square offices I was reminded of a remark by Jørn Utzon. Explaining the thin-shell concrete vaults of his Bagsværd Church in Denmark, he observed that they offer "the reassurance of something above your head which is built, not just designed". This remark goes to the core of the tectonic tradition of architecture espoused by Viollet-le-Duc, Mies van der Rohe and Louis Kahn which forms the bedrock of the Bennetts office. In Devonshire Square, you are confronted by a structure that is satisfyingly robust, its column and beam junctions clear, the webs of the I-beams neatly and visibly stiffened. As with all Bennetts' work, it is not designed merely to please the eye or camera, but to offer the deeper architectural pleasures that arise from the thoughtful making of form and space.

Such pleasures are a hallmark of the office's work, and all the more satisfying because the contingencies of contemporary construction and a growing preoccupation with gestural form-making and surface effects seem everywhere to militate against them. Refusing to reduce architecture to "the wrapping on a candy bar", the Bennetts office holds on to the belief that – to borrow Viollet-le-Duc's phrase, so rich in implications – "constructive processes" are the essential basis of the discipline.

PROJECTS A–F

BENNETTS ASSOCIATES' OFFICES
LONDON, 2001–02

Bennetts Associates has revitalised a group of redundant industrial buildings in Clerkenwell and has applied its expertise in sustainability and office planning to create a rich sequence of spaces and a stimulating working environment.

Hemmed in by Georgian or early Victorian terraces, the site has an irregular boundary and two existing buildings on either side of a small, cobbled courtyard. On the north side is a former printworks, once used as a foundry for cast metal lettering and more recently as the premises of a commercial printers. On the south side is a small eighteenth century barn, a unique survivor from the days when livestock required a resting place on their way to Smithfield Market. Between the barn and the boundary wall is a new, two-storey studio space, replacing some outbuildings that were beyond repair.

In design terms, the existing buildings are refurbished sensitively whilst being brought up to date with the requirements of a modern office, whereas the new elements are expressed as calm, low-profile additions in counterpoint to the disparate architectural styles.

Although the barn was in a state of near collapse, it has been restored to form the hub of Bennetts Associates' new offices, with its rugged brickwork exposed to view at every opportunity. Meeting rooms and the library are located in its three floors and refreshment points in the circulation route through the barn encourage interaction between the workspaces on either side. This leaves the whole of the printworks and the new extension free for open-plan space, with good levels of daylighting and a flexible arrangement of workstations that can be serviced from the floor. A double-height volume near the entrance serves as a meeting place for the whole office. The main entrance itself is through the existing wall on to Rawstorne Place, allowing the courtyard to retain its original dimensions and atmosphere.

By virtue of the barn's 'intervention' and the site's quirky shape, the experience of using the building is unlike any of the firm's larger projects, but the need for improvisation has not compromised its effectiveness as a workplace. The informal diversity of spaces and the pattern of movement that connects them create an exceptional working environment full of unexpected glimpses, colour, texture and light.

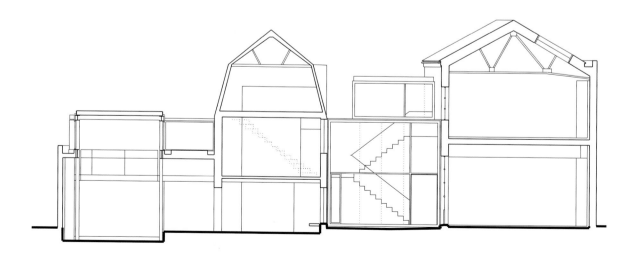

**Bennetts
Associates' Offices**
Above: The offices are
surrounded by residential
terraces. Sadlers Wells
theatre is visible in the
distance

Right: Location plan

Opposite, above: The
barn and courtyard,
before conversion

Opposite, below: Cross
section, with the barn in
the centre

St John Street

Rawstorne Street

**Bennetts
Associates' Offices**
Above: Junction of the
new studio and the barn

Above right: The new
studio space

Below: Ground and
first floor plan

Opposite: The courtyard,
viewed from the reception
area

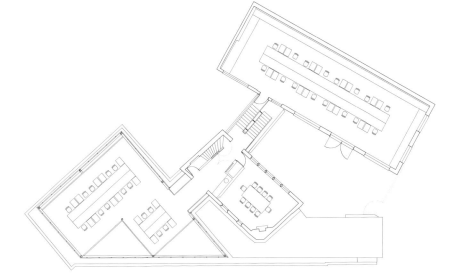

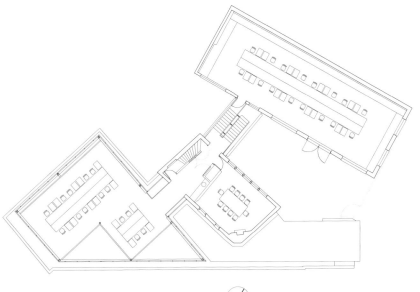

Bennetts Associates' Offices
Above: The first floor of the printworks

Opposite, above: Walls without windows are heavily insulated and lined with storage

Opposite, below: The barn appears as a piece of archaeology within the office

BT Edinburgh Park

Above: Night view of the amenity pavilion. The red cube contains conference rooms, kitchens, a boardroom suite and plant. Cafe and restaurant seating occupies the perimeter spaces

Below: The cafe at water level. The earlier John Menzies building is in the distance, partially obscured by the structure

Opposite: Typical floor plan (first). For site plan see John Menzies

BT EDINBURGH PARK
EDINBURGH, 1996–99

British Telecom's Scottish headquarters is the landmark building envisaged by Richard Meier's strict masterplan, terminating the western range of buildings at Edinburgh Park.

As part of BT's programme to rationalise its office space and working practices throughout the United Kingdom, this competition-winning design is a near neighbour to Bennetts Associates' earlier headquarters for John Menzies, completed in 1995. Occupying the business park's prime site, the main rectangular volume conforms to the alignment of buildings along a series of lochans, or small lakes. By way of a counterpoint, a cylindrical pavilion projecting into the lochan offers a sculptural and colourful contrast and a pivotal location for the restaurant, cafe and conference facilities.

The main building is rigorously organised into six parallel floorplates on each of three floors, connected laterally by circulation routes across their ends.

Although the office floorplates represent an evolution of the John Menzies and PowerGen projects, the multiplicity of non-office spaces provides a range of spatial experiences that is appropriate to the larger scale of the building and its 900 inhabitants. Three of the five atria between the floorplates are narrow and open-sided, so that they function as an informal extension to the workplace and a focal point for each pair of floorplates. The two wider atria are enclosed, partly to fulfil the need for fire breaks and future subdivision but mainly to establish a change of atmosphere. One is the busy main entrance, with security functions, glazed lifts and an open stair, whilst the other is a sanctuary from the workplace that takes the form of a quiet, internal garden. Binding the whole building together is the 'street', a full-height circulation space with spectacular views over the park and beyond to the Pentland Hills and Edinburgh Castle.

The cylindrical amenity pavilion is located at the intersection of the street and the main entrance atrium. At its centre, a saturated red colour defines rectilinear functions such as plantrooms, kitchens, meeting rooms and a boardroom suite. Seen through a transparent veil of solar shading and screens, the 'red cube' as it has become known is something of a beacon for drivers heading for the city's ring road.

A programme of public art by artists with Scottish connections is distributed throughout the building.

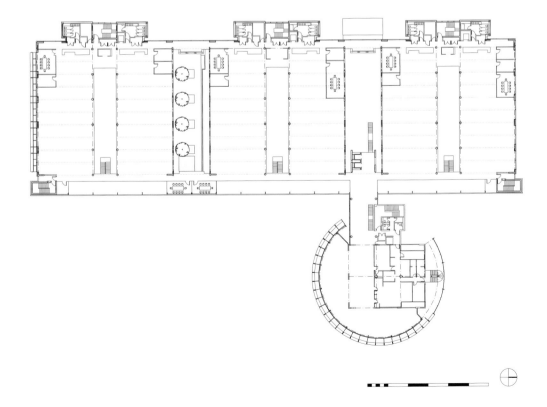

BT Edinburgh Park

Above: High quality in situ concrete is used to spatial effect in the workplace

Right: One of the two wider atrium spaces provides an internal garden

Opposite, above: The junction between the cylindrical amenity pavilion and the main building

Opposite, below (left): Concrete coffers have a tapering profile, allowing warm air to drift naturally into atrium spaces, where it is recirculated via the plantrooms above each core

Opposite, below (right): Reflected plan and section of structural bay. As with PowerGen and John Menzies, thermal mass is an essential part of the low energy strategy

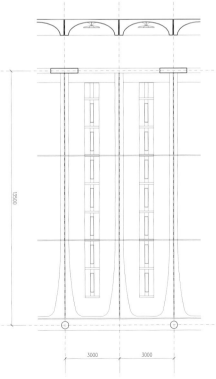

**Cass Business School,
City University**
Above: The school's entrance facade looks out on the City's financial district, whereas its brick facades face a largely residential area

Right: East-west section

Opposite, left: West elevation

Opposite, right: Second floor plan, showing multiple lecture rooms

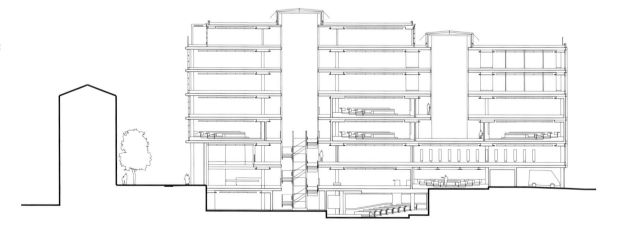

CASS BUSINESS SCHOOL, CITY UNIVERSITY
LONDON, 1999–2002

Aimed at fulfilling the University's ambition for "an intellectual hub" serving the City of London, this is Bennetts Associates' first substantial education building. The design connects the ideas of several previous projects in terms of urban design and internal planning to the requirements of a knowledge-based institution, where informal information transfer is as important as the formal teaching process.

The project is partly financed by the redevelopment of an entire city block masterplanned by Bennetts Associates, with commercial buildings towards the prime frontage on Chiswell Street and the business school in a less valuable but still prominent location in Bunhill Row.

Internally, the main floors of the building are dominated by two types of space that are contained within office-type dimensions for future flexibility. First, there are a dozen lecture rooms for up to 80 people, generally based on the Harvard principle of debate and interaction between lecturer and students in a U-shaped layout. Second, a series of large and small break out areas – located in and around atrium spaces, circulation routes and staircases – extend the learning process beyond the teaching spaces in a way that animates the school as a whole. As well as introducing light and colour, the atria and the broad circulation routes aid orientation in an environment largely comprising numerous separate rooms.

The lower levels contain a learning resource centre, cafe and a 180-seat lecture theatre, whilst the upper floors are devoted to offices for academic staff, a restaurant and a suite of rooms for executive teaching.

Away from its main entrance on Bunhill Row, the building makes a virtue of its irregularly shaped plot by placing a variety of informal spaces within a curving, brick-panelled facade. In so doing, the building addresses the localised 'shift' in the townscape between its commercial and residential neighbours and signifies through its architectural language that this is an educational facility rather than another office building.

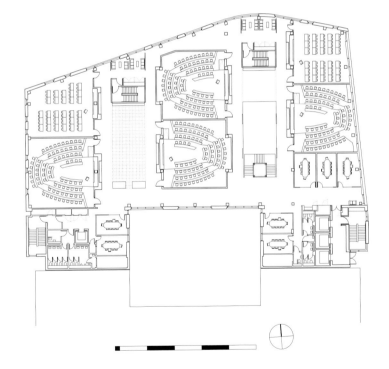

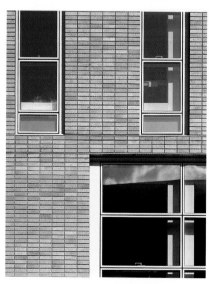

**Cass Business School,
City University**
Left and above, left:
Views of the learning
resource centre

Above, right: The main
lecture hall in the
basement

Below: North elevation

Opposite, above: One
of the two atria spaces

Opposite, below:
Facade detail

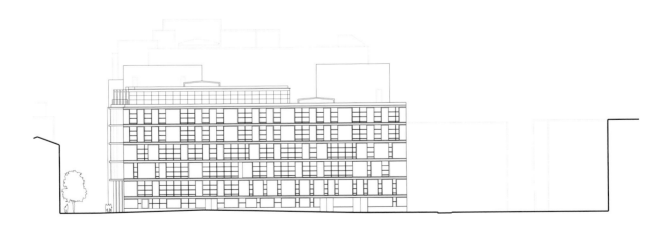

CENTRAL LIBRARY AND
JUBILEE STREET DEVELOPMENT
BRIGHTON, 1999–2005

Brighton and Hove's new library is the centrepiece of a regeneration project that stitches back together the fragmented streets of the North Laines area near the city centre.

Two previous attempts to build a new library had foundered during the planning process so, when the Council was obliged by the Government to follow the Private Finance Initiative (PFI) for the third attempt, it made design quality a central feature of the tendering procedure. Developers were invited to bid for the whole of the Jubilee Street site, with the prospect of cross-subsidising the library with revenue from other developments. The scheme devised by Bennetts Associates, working with local firm Lomax Cassidy & Edwards, was chosen after an extensive public consultation exercise and has since been praised as a rare example of high design quality within the PFI system.

The masterplan reinstates Jubilee Street to its original alignment, with most of the new buildings playing a background role in order that the external spaces predominate. Street level is filled with shops, cafes and restaurants, with either offices or residential above. In the centre of the site, a small square provides the setting for the library and a venue for public art, performance and the Brighton Festival. With a hotel on its south side and a cafe on its east, the square also resolves the unfortunate approach to a 1970s municipal swimming pool.

The library adopts a formal plan, with activities that require enclosure around the perimeter on three sides and the main reading room/reference library in the centre, where it strikes up a direct relationship with the square outside. The intention is that this should feel like a civic building of importance – a place of repose and presence – as if to demonstrate that modern libraries are not wholly devoted to computers or are made obsolete by the internet.

The engineering of the building meticulously supports the architectural intention. The thick walls surrounding the central space contain air ducts from the roof-level plantrooms, feeding air through voids in the concrete floorslabs before entering the perimeter rooms and the main space. In winter, warm air is recirculated back to the plantroom at high level; in summer, the extract system is driven by three centrally located wind towers, adding spice to the skyline of a city known for its Regency domes and minarets. Dominating the library, eight freestanding concrete columns with fan-shaped heads support the middle floor and the roof, defining the character of the space and greatly adding to the building's thermal mass. Lightweight bridges cross the air-gap between the central structure and the deep reveals of its enclosure.

As with previous buildings like PowerGen, environmental engineering is the Trojan horse for structural and spatial expression.

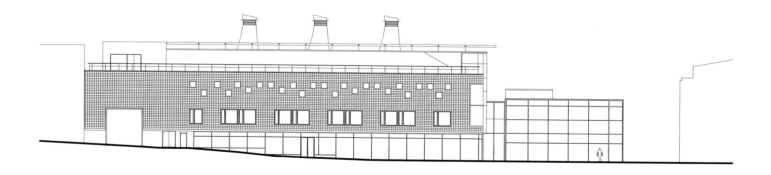

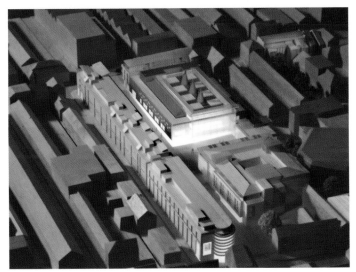

**Central Library
and Jubilee Street
Development**

Above: View from the
new square to the library

Far left: Development
masterplan model

Left: The corner window
above the entrance

Opposite, below: Jubilee
Street elevation

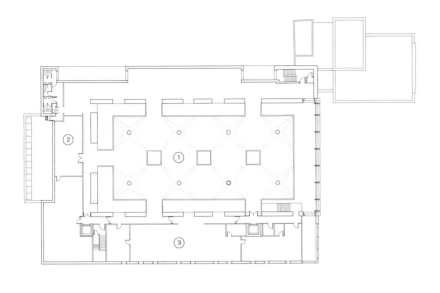

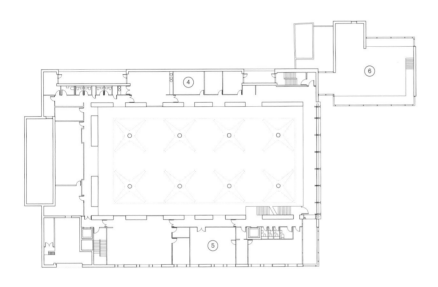

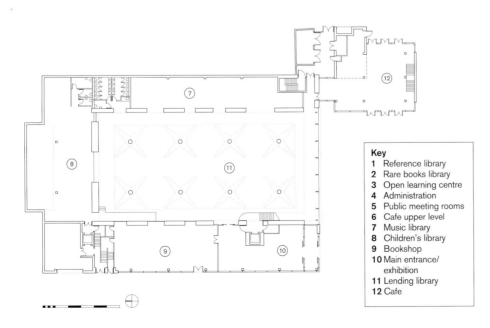

Key
1 Reference library
2 Rare books library
3 Open learning centre
4 Administration
5 Public meeting rooms
6 Cafe upper level
7 Music library
8 Children's library
9 Bookshop
10 Main entrance/ exhibition
11 Lending library
12 Cafe

Central Library and Jubilee Street Development
Top: Detail of the 'floating' central structure

Above: The main reference and lending library space

Left (from top): Second; first (mezzanine); and ground floor plans

Opposite: One of the eight free-standing columns

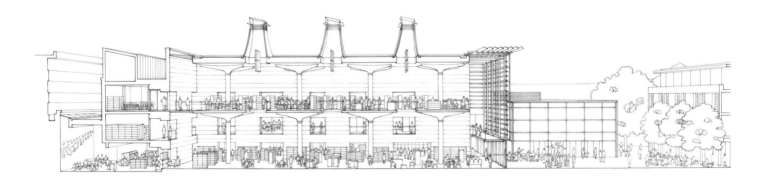

**Central Library
and Jubilee Street
Development**
Top, left: The main space,
glimpsed from the
mezzanine floor
circulation

Top, right: Corner details

Above: North-south
section showing the wind
towers on the roof and
the new square on the
right

Opposite: The lending
library

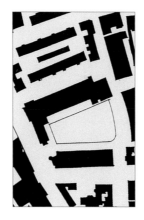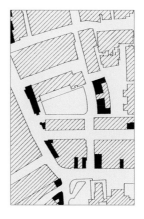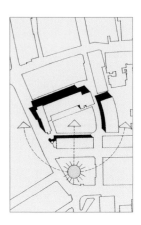

CHANNEL 4 HEADQUARTERS COMPETITION
LONDON, 1990

Bennetts Associates had been established for three years when it was shortlisted alongside Richard Rogers Partnership and Stirling Wilford for Channel 4 Television's headquarters in central London.

At the time, Channel 4 was located in a lively street near the West End, whereas its new location was quiet and semi-derelict. Bennetts Associates felt that Channel 4 might find the move to a new headquarters a stark contrast to their existing location, so the competition scheme was intended to inject the site with lively activities beyond the requirements of the brief. Based on an historical analysis of the area, the overall strategy for the competition scheme reinstated the former street pattern, introduced street life to the area and created a new public park at the centre of the new site.

All the windowless studio space for the television company was located below ground, making full use of an existing deep basement across the whole site. At the upper levels, administrative offices, cafes and restaurants were placed around the edges of the site, with a linear atrium providing orientation and a daylit focus for the basement areas below. A five-storey entrance pavilion formed a transitional space for Channel 4's public activities between the busy main road and the park.

This was the first substantial urban project examined by Bennetts Associates and it allowed the firm to develop ideas that have surfaced many times since. The primary intention was to repair a long neglected piece of downtown Westminster and suggest that streets and public spaces were at least as important as a major new building. The proposals also stressed the importance of a high quality workplace and, although the building itself was relatively assertive, it consciously avoided the notion of an iconic object that was isolated from its context.

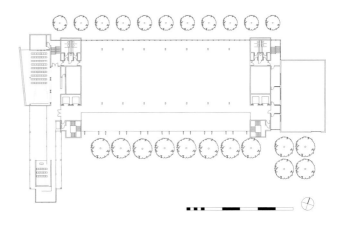

Channel 4 Headquarters competition
Above: Typical plan

Left: Interior perspective

Opposite, above: Site analysis diagrams: existing site; reinstating street lines; figure ground; cafes and shops; sunpath

Opposite, below: Perspective from Horseferry Road

CITY INN WESTMINSTER
LONDON, 1999–2003

The design aims to reconcile a highly repetitive, 460-bedroom hotel with the constraints and variations of its urban context by expressive massing, lively public spaces and a new pedestrian thoroughfare.

Hemmed in by Government office buildings, a block of private flats and the car park serving the Millbank Tower, the site was vacant for many years prior to redevelopment. In consequence, the form of the building makes the least possible impact on the established rights to views and daylight of neighbouring properties and maintains natural ventilation to the car park.

In response to the potential for a lively townscape and the need for internal legibility,

the hotel's volume is divided into several parts above a two-storey podium. Separate bedroom wings of different heights are connected by a visually distinct lift tower that resolves the acute angle between the two main blocks and animates the skyline. As a way of enriching the building's profile, cantilevered canopies above the bedroom blocks conceal the rooftop plantrooms and provide a degree of solar shading to the fully glazed top floor suites.

At ground level, the project introduces a new pedestrian thoroughfare between John Islip Street and Millbank, allowing not only an extensive frontage for the restaurant and cafe but also a substantial opportunity for public art. With the support of Westminster City Council and the Tate Gallery, the

pedestrian street has been designed in collaboration with the artist Susanna Heron, with the intention of creating a series of powerful installations for a new urban route originating at the Thames Embankment. The continuous, solid wall that provides the backdrop to Heron's work also serves as the visual screen to the adjacent car park.

The public areas are complemented by a 'skylounge' perched between the main lift motor rooms on the fifteenth floor, with spectacular views over central London.

City Inn Westminster
Right: Typical floor plan

Opposite: View from John Islip Street. Principal cladding materials are blue glazed terracotta and aluminium

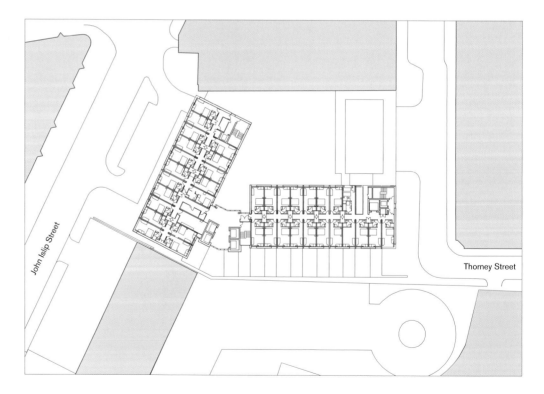

City Inn Westminster
Above, left: The main entrance

Above, right: A corner bedroom, overlooking the Thames

Below: East-west section

Opposite, above: View from the south side of the River Thames

Opposite, below (left): The new pedestrian thoroughfare

Opposite, below (right): Reception spaces

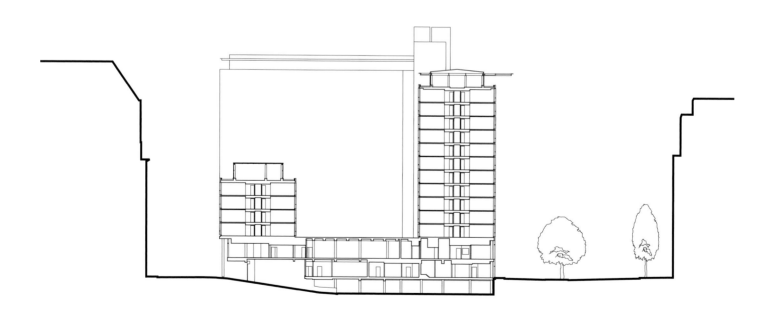

City Place Offices

Right: North-south section. The top floor is like a tall attic under the sloping roof. Lower floors have vaulted concrete structures

Below right: Typical floor plan

Opposite: The principal elevation, seen from the central square of City Place. Side and rear elevations have less glazing, between bands of standing seam metal cladding

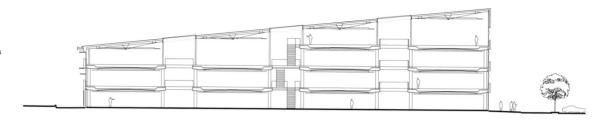

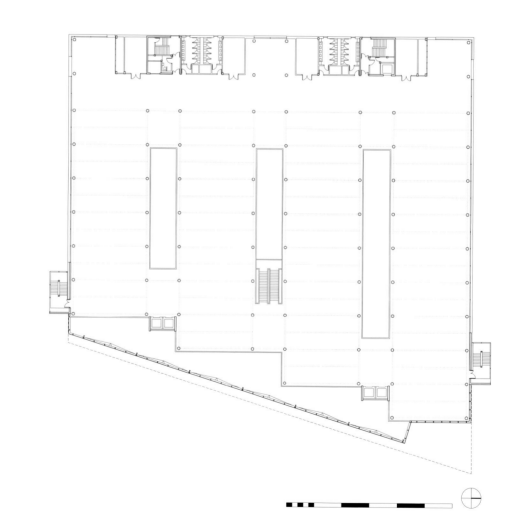

CITY PLACE OFFICES
GATWICK, 1999–2002

This project illustrates the continual evolution of Bennetts Associates' ideas about space, structure and environment and is an early sign that the development sector is beginning to adopt the ideas pioneered in owner-occupied buildings.

BAA's office park next to the airport occupies the site of the original 1930s airfield, where passenger aircraft pulled up on the grass outside a circular, two-storey pavilion that had since been converted to business space. In response, Bennetts Associates proposed a radical change to the layout of the whole site, which had been planned in the 1980s but had yet to commence construction, so that the first new building could adopt a sympathetic form alongside its listed neighbour.

The envelope of the building takes the form of a trapezium both in plan and in section, allowing a change in scale and alignment out of respect for the pavilion and a new public square at the heart of the business park. Within this angular enclosure, the irregular space created between four parallel floorplates and the perimeter is used to create amenity areas or circulation zones whereas, below the sloping roof, the top floors take the form of a broad and lofty attic.

The east end facing the square is entirely glazed, whilst the main service/stair cores form a buffer zone at the building's west end where the view is restricted.

The basic unit of the workplace manipulates the characteristics of an energy-efficient building to create a synthesis of space, structure and environment, where no single component can be removed without affecting the whole. Although the building is densely occupied, heat gains are limited by careful solar control, so that full air-conditioning is unnecessary. This enables a combination of thermal mass, chilled panels and air supplied from the floor to provide comfortable working conditions and ensures that the structure remains the dominant spatial device.

In a development of previous projects, the vaulted floor slabs are made of precast concrete units spanning 13.5 metres, with a chilled panel/lighting raft in each of the precast vaulted concrete coffers.

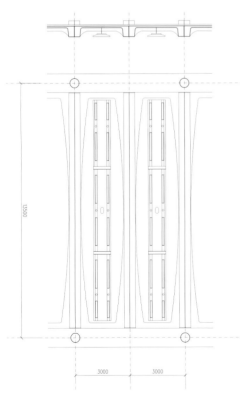

City Place offices
Above: The lofty top floor

Left: Vaulted concrete slabs with service rafts

Far left: Reflected plan and section of vaulted precast concrete units, with service rafts. The service rafts include chilled beams, lighting, smoke detectors and PA system

Opposite: Steel is used for the glazing and roof structure, to distinguish them from the concrete floorplates

City Road Basin

Above: Computer montage of the planning application scheme. Bennetts Associates is responsible for the tower on the left

Left: The basin before development

Opposite, left: The masterplan, showing low-rise terraces parallel to the basin and two towers at the junction with City Road. Existing buildings are shaded

Opposite, right: Model of the masterplan, before design development on individual sites

CITY ROAD BASIN
LONDON, 2003 –

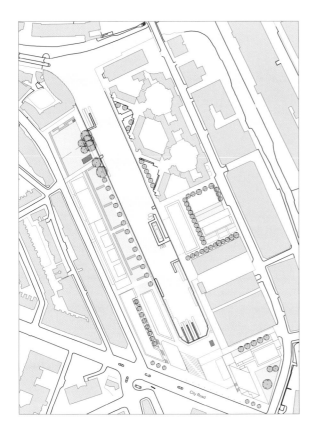

Regeneration of the land and waterways around City Road Basin in Islington follows decades of industrial decline along the length of the Regent's Canal.

Commissioned jointly by Islington Council, British Waterways and a number of landowners, Bennetts Associates' masterplan creates a high-density, mixed-tenure residential development that opens the basin up to public use, with parks and walkways around the water and a range of lively commercial and community uses at ground level. The placement of two towers at the point where the basin meets City Road provides the strongest possible change of identity for the basin area and a metaphorical gateway to one of Islington's largest but previously undiscovered amenities.

The greater density at City Road means that lower scale buildings and a variety of open spaces are possible elsewhere on the site. A boat club for local schoolchildren and moorings for narrowboats support leisure activity on the canal, whilst the terraced area at the head of the basin not only disguises an electricity substation but is also the venue for occasional performances and other events.

Since the masterplan was approved by the planning authorities in 2004, various architects have made detailed proposals for individual buildings and Bennetts Associates' design for the eastern tower develops the complementary relationship between the two principal buildings established at masterplan stage. Using the angular geometry of the site as its generator, the plan of the tower

comprises a right-angled triangle set against a thin rectangle, each volume rising to different heights to dramatise the skyline.

As with some previous projects in sensitive areas, extensive public consultation before and during the design process was essential to receiving public support and proved to be a natural extension to Bennetts Associates' open and collaborative approach to design. The firm's continuing role also includes co-ordination of all the public areas around the basin.

CUMMINS ENGINE COMPANY
KENT, 1996–98

Right: Upper ground
level plan. Offices are
to the right and test
cells to the left of the
production space

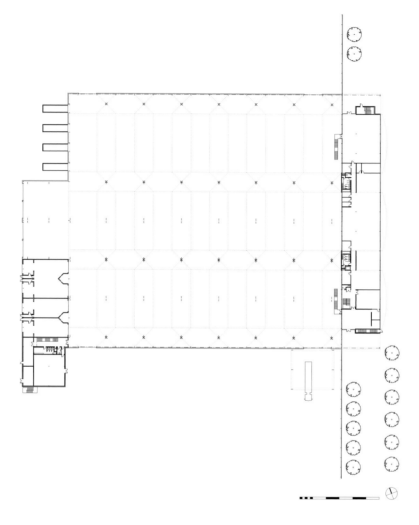

This project is an architectural rarity –
a substantial industrial building for an
enlightened client, where the quality of the
space and working environment supports
the manufacturing process.

Cummins Engine Company, an American
multi-national company with a distinguished
architectural portfolio around the world,
required an assembly plant for diesel-powered
generator sets weighing up to 60 tonnes.
Bennetts Associates' analysis of the project
extended to the assembly line itself and helped
to rework the layout of its main functions so
that the new building could cater for alternative
production operations in rapidly changing
market conditions.

The resulting 15,000 square metre project
comprises 12,000 square metres of factory
space in a single tall space, with three
floors of associated offices at one end and
a heavily-serviced group of engine test cells
at the other. The production space in the
centre is therefore free of all obstructions
except wide-spaced columns and can expand
laterally, with production lines and travelling
cranes arranged either north-south or east-
west as required.

The structural grid of steel 'trees', arranged
on a 28.8 x 14.4 metre grid to suit typical
production layouts, carries the roof
independently of any crane rail structures
that may change in future. The roof itself
is barrel-vaulted in three bays and its glazed
apex floods the workplace with daylight,
suggesting a sense of grandeur appropriate
to its enormous scale and high quality
working conditions. Ribbon windows at
low level and the reflected light from the
clean, white floor make the production areas
suitable for meeting spaces and team areas
directly beside the assembly lines.

Because of the gently sloping terrain,
entry for personnel and visitors is at the
middle floor of the offices, where there is
a commanding view over the factory interior.
The change in levels is accentuated by a
steel-framed plane of glass or galvanised
mesh that passes right through the building,
providing visual screening for delivery areas
on the main approach to the building.
Internally, its transparency emphasises the
company's philosophical connection between
administrative and production functions.

Cummins Engine Company

Above: The production space seen from the office entrance. Temporary crane rail structures are grey, permanent building structures are white. Moving elements are yellow. As an indication of the large scale, a man is just visible on one of the 36-litre diesel engines

Left: The side aisle to the production space

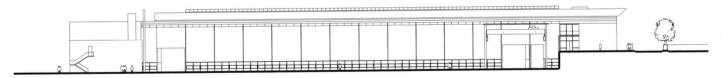

Cummins Engine Company
Top: Night view from upper ground level

Above: South elevation, with office entrance on the right and test cells on the left

Opposite: The production space, showing services running above the steel 'trees'

Cummins Engine Company

Above, left: Profiled metal cladding above ribbon window at floor level

Left: The approach to the main entrance

Opposite, top: Natural ventilation through opening windows at floor level is enhanced in summer by opening rooflights

Opposite, below: Cross section

DEVONSHIRE SQUARE OFFICES
CITY OF LONDON, 1996–2002

Bennetts Associates' appointment for this 30,000 square metre office building came at a time when the firm was executing a series of headquarters offices on out-of-town sites, using concrete as the principal structural medium. However, the last 20 years had seen steel become the dominant structural medium in the City of London on account of its potential for rapid construction and prefabrication for congested sites. At Devonshire Square, Bennetts Associates set out to reconcile its rational approach to design and construction with a highly constrained urban site adjacent to a series of listed buildings.

The practice's strategy uses the placement of structures, services and circulation cores, atrium spaces, entrances and corners to create a relatively complex architectural composition that retains its capacity for a highly functional workplace.

To achieve this and retain a sense of integrity, the major cores are placed at the perimeter, leaving the centre of each floor free for the wide, adaptable floors required in major City office buildings. In consequence, the cores play a significant role in the townscape, forming landmarks at key views and junctions without the limitations imposed by regular office fenestration. In addition, the corners of the building are marked by a change in scale and construction, helping to dictate the location of conference rooms and, in the case of the northwest corner, the main entrance.

Unlike some of the classic exposed steel frame buildings in the United States, where a handsome external frame can disguise a concrete-encased structure inside, the external structure at Devonshire Square has the integrity of its load-bearing function. To express this, the columns and beams on the facade are not covered with fire protection,

but are shielded by the cladding design. The column flanges and the beams – the dimensions of which are large enough to cover the raised floor and ceiling zone – incorporate a degree of redundancy in the structure that assists with fire resistance. The necessary thermal break between each internal beam and the external structure is achieved by a special insulated connection. Tolerances are about half that of a normal steel frame and workmanship on the facade itself is of a very high order.

The need for artificial cooling in the IT-intensive office floors was evident from the outset and, in consequence, the four-pipe fan coil system follows fairly conventional lines. Nevertheless, measures to control solar gain include external louvres on the south elevation and in-cavity blinds on those facades subject to low sun angles.

**Devonshire
Square Offices**
Right: Site plan.
Devonshire Square
is to the top left

Opposite: View from
Houndsditch

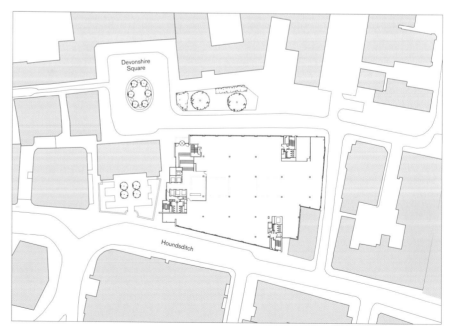

**Devonshire
Square Offices**
Above, left to right:
Structural steel assembly
on site

Left: Detail of load-
bearing steel facade

Below: Cross section,
with Houndsditch on the
right and a tube line on
the left. The upper floors
are conventional office
space, the first and
second floors are deep
plan space for financial
trading

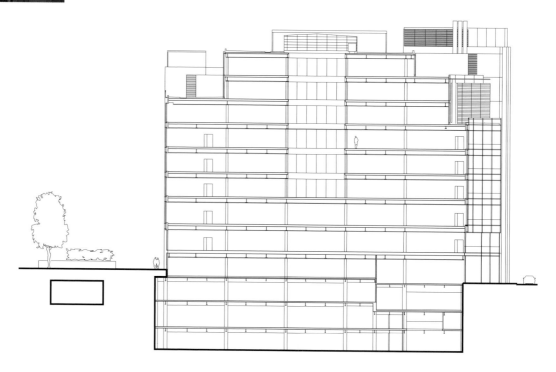

**Devonshire
Square Offices**
Above: The main
staircase

Left: Detail of corner
to Devonshire Square

EXHIBITION BUILDING COMPETITION
SOUTHERN ENGLAND, 2003

Exhibition Building Competition
Above: Distant view showing the exhibition hall rising above existing aircraft hangars

Below: Landscape masterplan, based on the pattern of runways for the former airfield

Opposite, above: The exhibition hall, with the existing hangar to the right

Opposite, below: Section, with existing hangar to the left

A strong emphasis on sustainability underpins this competition proposal, which places a large exhibition hall on a disused airfield alongside several existing hangars that are to be retained as stores. The supporting strategy for the downland site includes policies for landscape, buildings and transport that aim for carbon neutral impact on the environment.

The 30,000 square metre building is closely coupled to a curved landform created from the broken-up runways, concealing a labyrinth of ventilation routes to cool incoming air. Coppiced planting extends from the top of this embankment into the landscape to provide a substantial biomass energy resource, harvested on a three year cycle and converted to usable heat in boilers. The main structure for the hall is timber, with a catenary formed out of plywood sheeting and cables for the main roof. The high point of the catenary corresponds with the main public circulation galleries and a series of ground level connections with the retained aircraft hangars.

The low profile of the exhibition hall roof and planted embankment to the south contrast with the building's glazed north wall, which overlooks a nearby town and reveals some of the large-scale exhibits to a distant view.

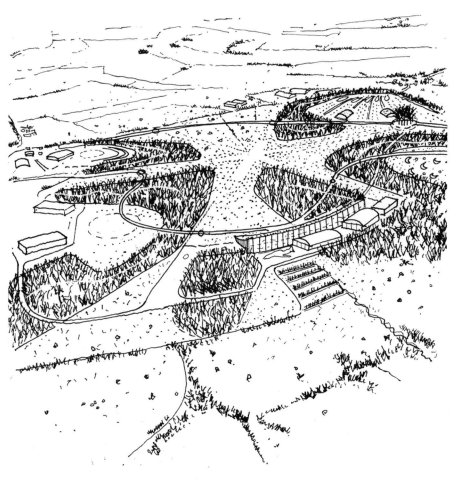

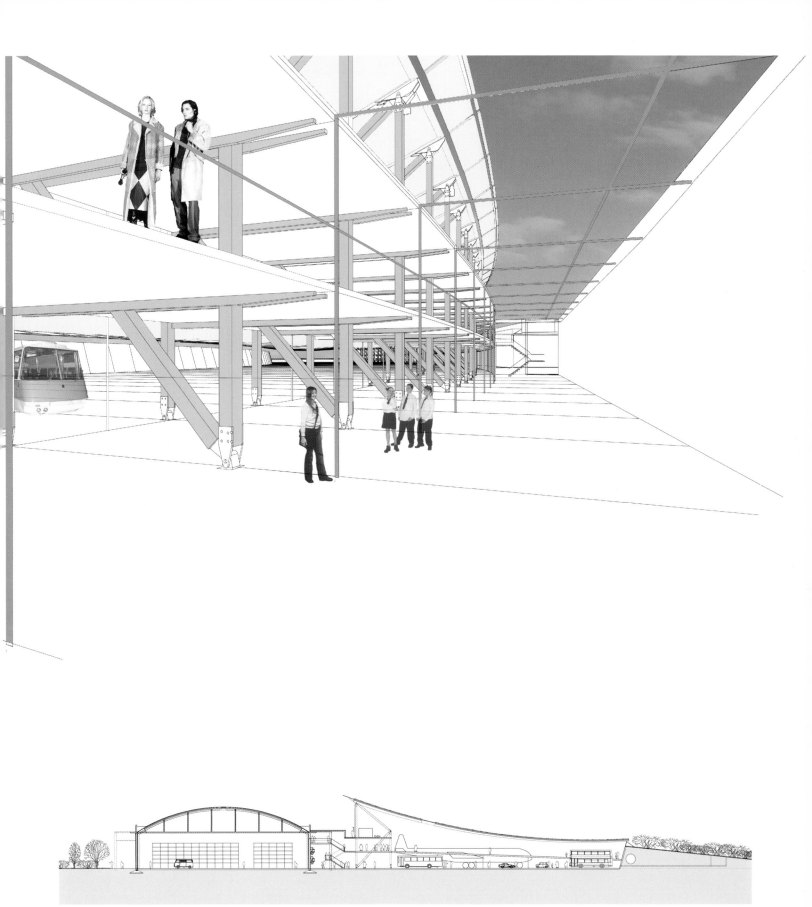

FRANCIS DUFFY
PROCESS

Bennetts Associates' appointment for the Royal Shakespeare Theatre in Stratford-upon-Avon and the completion of its Central Library in Brighton early in 2005 belie a reputation that first came to prominence on headquarters buildings and City of London offices. The extent of this diverse range of projects is evident from the individual project descriptions elsewhere in this book but, here, Francis Duffy describes a consistent design process that underpins all the firm's work. He goes on to assess its application to his own specialist subject – the workplace and its history – and graphically illustrates his thesis by highlighting the anatomical characteristics of 11 buildings by Bennetts Associates. In doing so, he makes the case for offices as good architecture, historically neglected in the United Kingdom but now forming the staple diet of many leading architects.

2

PowerGen Headquarters
Right: Atrium detail,
looking towards the
office floors

Introduction

25 years ago for one British architect to describe another as a specialist in office design would be immediately understood by the majority of his colleagues as a sly euphemism for a hack, a degraded fellow, an unoriginal and probably incompetent money grubber, a lackey in the pay of unscrupulous and philistine developers. Things have changed. In fact today Bennetts Associates has rather the opposite problem. The practice is anxious not to be typecast as designers of office buildings precisely because it has become so well known for a particularly strong and original series of contributions to the revitalisation of office design that has been such an interesting and unexpected feature of British architecture in the last two and a half decades. Bennetts Associates wants the world to know that it can apply the original and rigorous briefing and design process which has been so effective in their work on offices to *any* architectural problem in *any* building type.

Bennetts Associates has reversed another pattern that had long been taken for granted in British architectural practice. The classic route to success for young practices is still to achieve early recognition through winning architectural competitions for non commercial public buildings, often arts projects, and then, usually much later, to be granted access to large scale commercial commissions such as designing office buildings. Bennetts Associates' trajectory has been the opposite, moving from their brilliant initial successes in office design to tackling an ever-widening variety of projects in both the public and private sectors.

This essay weaves together four parallel and interconnected stories. The first is the importance of the practice's love of process, particularly its rigorous modes of enquiry and highly disciplined design skills, on making architectural sense out of the changing workplace. The second is the historical context of the rediscovery in the UK in the last two decades of the office as a building type worthy of serious consideration by the very best British architects. The third is an account of the very specific and important part that Bennetts Associates has played in this rediscovery. The fourth is a sketch of the opportunities that new developments in office design are opening up to practices such as Bennetts Associates.

In some ways it has been the firm's good fortune to have been in the right place at the right time – the UK since the mid-1980s has been a very fertile place in terms of office design – but, as the Roman poet Virgil demonstrated long ago, it is not enough to find the golden bough. The opportunity has to be turned into action. It is necessary not only to glimpse a glinting opportunity hidden in the dark woods but also to grasp the prize with an appropriate degree of intelligence, agility, decisiveness and imagination.

The rediscovery of the office building is an important part of the development of Bennetts Associates. What exactly has the practice contributed to office design? In this analysis the following questions are addressed:

– How does Bennetts Associates' office design compare with what has been achieved by other architects in the same period?

- Why is it so much better than so much British office architecture of previous decades?
- How does it compare with international office design of the same period?
- How robust a platform does this body of work provide for anticipating the emerging requirements of the increasingly virtual and mobile knowledge economy?

The answers to these questions throw a great deal of incidental light on the processes that are necessary to produce buildings of the highest quality for demanding clients during periods of radical change.

The importance of process in creating thoroughbred architecture

Bennetts Associates' unusually thorough and well-articulated briefing and design process has contributed enormously to its success. The three salient characteristics of this process are: first, an insistence on analysis before design; second, the collaborative nature of the design process and; third, an inclusive attitude towards construction and delivery. It goes without saying that the purpose of process is always to produce architecture of the highest quality.

The practice has resisted the common architectural tendency to conjure an image or a concept out of thin air without first thoroughly understanding the problems and opportunities that face their clients. In this way the practice avoids superficiality and is enabled to design buildings that have a far better chance of working for the long term. The resulting architecture has the resolution that is the hallmark of an in-depth understanding of purpose.

This process evolved early, its value being demonstrated on Bennetts Associates' first major building, Imperium, an office development in Reading. Having been given a one-page brief by the developer client, the practice's response was to draw diagrams of each major part of the project – the context, the site, the office space, the floorplates, the cores. Each of these components was examined in turn. The presentation and review of alternative options facilitated discussion with the client although it was always made clear which were the practice's preferences and why. The same process was applied to purely visual options when appropriate. The final result

Bennetts Associates' Offices
Far left: Detail of new studio space

Middle left: Ground floor meeting room in the barn

Left: Reception area and barn viewed from the courtyard

was a strong, rational building in which all parts work in unison. The test of success was that no single element can be removed or changed without diminishing the whole. All parties were involved in this process of exploration – engineers, quantity surveyors as well as the client – and everyone was able to see how his or her views, priorities and recommendations had been carefully considered and, if successful, to appreciate how they had been incorporated in the final solution. In effect, in this process the lead architect acts as a superior kind of editor. Astonishingly, Imperium's client said it was the first time an architect had really explained to him what the brief for speculative offices actually meant. This successful experience made Bennetts Associates confident that a rational process was essential to produce good architecture.

The Bennetts Associates process has greatly developed over time but is still essentially the same for nearly all the practice's projects. One important consequence is that it is impossible for one member of the design team to monopolise design decisions. When design studies are put forward for round-table brainstorming, there is no prior agenda and no-one is allowed to be possessive about his or her ideas especially if they do not correspond to the overall design direction. The lead architect's function as quasi-editor is to capture the best ideas from whatever source while constantly checking that the design as it develops always remains on target to meet the client's requirements.

The initial sketch for a project is likely to be a diagram or, even better, several diagrams drawn by different team members. The first purely architectural concept might not emerge for some time as these diagrams are collated and compared. In fact the practice's clear preference is to steer clear of formal architectural solutions for as long as possible. Design concepts often do not emerge until many models have been made and many diagrams drawn. For the same reason computer drawings are resisted at the early stages of design. White card or foam models are considered to be better than 3-D computer visualisations. The eventual design direction that emerges often confounds everyone's preconceptions. Debating the strengths and weaknesses of the options is an essential part of establishing a workable strategy. Most important of all the brief is usually written while this highly collaborative design is in progress. In other words, at Bennetts Associates design itself is considered to be an exploratory

process and is an essential part of helping clients to discover and articulate their brief.

While collaboration is the main characteristic of this process, it is also important to understand that agreement can only be achieved through empowerment. All members of the design team are encouraged to own the design as a whole through constant reinforcement and recognition of their individual contributions. This is also true of the conduct of the practice as a whole. Younger team members are encouraged to meet clients, consultants and contractors. There is no attempt to restrict such experiences to a select few. The result is that everyone's career development is accelerated while the practice as a whole benefits from increasing experience and low staff turnover. Younger architects are expected to learn, to mature and to become part of Bennetts Associates' long-term infrastructure. This is very different from the hire-and-fire culture prevalent in some other design-led firms.

There are now several centres of activity within the practice and the founders are no longer involved in every project. However, the design process is still firmly inclusive. Since it needs several people to make the process work, it is not considered right to credit any one building to any one individual, despite the media's love of doing exactly that. In fact, in completed buildings it is usually impossible to determine whose ideas are where since they are all so interwoven.

The office as a building type

In order to understand why this calm, rational, iterative and integrative process has been so important for the practice's work in office design at a particular moment in the history of the office as a building type, it is first necessary to be aware of its origins and nature.

The office as a distinct building type is an essentially late-nineteenth and twentieth century phenomenon, created by two related movements: the invention of bureaucracy and the application of the mechanical and industrially based principles of Scientific Management or Taylorism to office work.

Chicago, especially after the great fire in 1871, was the city that took maximum advantage of whatever technologies came to hand to push forward the development of the commercial office building. The rebuilding of the city gave exceptional opportunities to a remarkable group of planners, architects and engineers – William Le Baron

Jenney, Dankmar Adler, Daniel Burnham, Louis Sullivan and the greatest of them all, Frank Lloyd Wright.

In this international and historical context even the splendid Economist building in London's West End designed by the Smithsons in the early 1960s is clearly revealed more as a wistful glance backwards to the pioneering masterpieces of late-nineteenth century Chicago than as a serious competitor with the finest mid-twentieth century achievements of the North American office building tradition: the technically highly advanced and completely magnificent architectural confidence expressed by Mies van der Rohe and Philip Johnson's Seagram Building in New York, 1958, SOM's Inland Steel Building in Chicago, 1958, Union Carbide Building in New York, 1960, Saarinen's John Deere Headquarters in Moline, Illinois, 1964, or Kevin Roche and John Dinkeloo's Ford Foundation Building in New York, 1967. No contemporary commercial London office architectural practice could ever have claimed to be in the same league as the firms that produced these buildings.

The underlying processes that were developed in North America to achieve such successful offices designs and which were largely unknown or misunderstood in the UK are still highly relevant in today's very different world of work. Essentially there are two fundamental disciplines: firstly, the design, constructional and project management skills that are necessary to produce easily constructed, uncomplicated building shells that are robust enough to accommodate many diverse office uses over very long periods of time and, secondly, the highly political brief writing and data handling skills that are necessary to respond to and accommodate the much shorter term, constantly changing but nevertheless vitally important business requirements and work patterns of each commercial occupier. Office organisations are very complex but their needs relate directly and managerially to the design of office buildings and office interiors with a consistency and completeness that are rare in other building types. A sociological as well as an architectural imagination is needed to design offices successfully.

British office design 25 years ago
British office design had never produced anything to compare with Chicago's world famous architectural heroes, just as the contemporary British economy never grew at anything like the same spectacular rate.

**Bennetts
Associates' Offices**
Far left: The converted
printworks

Roche Dinkeloo
Middle left: Ford
Foundation, New York,
1967

The Smithsons
Left: Economist Building,
London,1964

No nineteenth century British city sprang like Chicago from the ashes nor reinvented itself in the same architecturally innovative way. Inter war offices in the UK were heavily influenced by North American innovations in many ways but tended to be architecturally retrogressive and apologetic as if accommodating office functions was not really what British cities were meant to be about.

Even after the destruction of the Second World War, when London really did have to be rebuilt, the resulting crop of new office buildings was stunted, under serviced and amateurish by American standards, reflecting more accurately British developers' ingenious but perversely opportunistic manipulation of planning controls than any technical competence or confidence in the office function as an important part of the economy.

Nor did Britain replicate until two decades later the various processes and divisions of professional labour that were absolutely necessary to plan, to construct and to fit out such huge buildings for demanding and technically adept developers and for sophisticated and rapidly changing corporate tenants. Programming and space planning skills were first developed in the US. Specialised engineering firms were already available in the 1950s and 1960s in New York, Chicago and San Francisco who knew exactly how to design huge high-rise steel structures, large-scale air-conditioning systems and enormous banks of speedy and reliable elevators.

In contrast the processes by which British post war office buildings used to be briefed, procured, designed and managed were primitive. British office developers had a bad name – not without justice since they were usually entirely consumed by supply side interests with scant regard for the requirements of their tenants and no commitment at all to market or user research. Letting agents were little help. On the demand side Facilities Management was just beginning to be organised as a profession. Interior designers, who through sheer proximity should have been in a position to understand tenants' needs, were marginal at best and, if noticed, were often considered to be ditzy and incompetent.

The structural reasons for this highly unsatisfactory situation were partly political. Perhaps the most important, given the generally socialist background at that time of the UK, was a built in bias against white collar office work. Such work was assumed *a priori* to be unnecessary, superficial, parasitic or even inevitably fraudulent. Hence the provision of office accommodation was given small priority compared with the self evidently justifiable demands of the health service, education and, of course, the blue collar production of revenue generating hardware. Although the American management theorist Peter Drucker had already coined the term in the early 1960s, the notion of the 'knowledge worker' is still to this day, even in architectural circles, a very long way from being in common currency.

A turning point

Just after the mid-century the high tide of American economic imperialism had reached its most magnificent architectural expression not only in the United States but throughout the entire Western world, and in fact wherever American economic power reached. Subsequently many new influences have reshaped office design, such as ideas and values from socially democratic Northern Europe, as well as the realisation of the potential inherent in rapid developments in information technology, and perhaps most important of all the new, non linear work processes and more fluid forms of business culture that are now superseding mechanistic Taylorist and Fordist models. Another most important set of new influences on office design has sprung from increasingly serious concerns about the environmental sustainability of a building type which consumes so much energy in itself and generates such extravagant commuting patterns. In consequence office design today is now no longer so strongly dominated by North American practice. By a completely unexpected turn of fate innovation in office design is more often to be found elsewhere, not least, in the UK.

The impact of these new social, technological and environmental influences on office design, within the context of the UK, has been quite fundamental: i.e. nothing less than the rediscovery in the early 1980s of the office as a building type worthy of serious architectural attention. Given the circumstances – since nothing much worse than contemporary British office accommodation could have hardly been imagined in an advanced economy – reinvention had to start from a very low base. However, while office design in the 1970s was still thought by most leading British architects to be of marginal importance, there were already exceptions such as Yorke Rosenberg

Richard Rogers
Far left: Lloyds of London,
City of London, 1986

Arup Associates
Left: Wiggins Teape
Headquarters,
Basingstoke, 1983

Sophos Headquarters
Right: View of office floor
and atrium circulation

and Mardell and Arup Associates with their strong American corporate connections. By the late 1970s and early 1980s the much more conspicuously innovative office designs of a generation of a younger generation of architects had begun to appear, in particular Norman Foster and Richard Rogers.

The reasons that the UK in general and London in particular have been relatively much more fruitful environments for office design to flourish in the last two decades are complex. The first and perhaps most important is the UK's intermediate position between the strong North American influences already described and the very different Northern European Social Democratic influences which have shaped Scandinavian, German and Dutch office architecture in ways that are responsive to individual user needs in terms of privacy, individual environmental control and ergonomics as well as increasingly to the macro issues of sustainability. The second and perhaps most spectacular reason, at least in the short term, was the sudden and shocking realisation in the UK in the early 1980s of the potential scale of the impact on office design of powerful, robust and ubiquitous information technology, an insight that was quickly to lead to the premature obsolescence of so many older office buildings. This shock was acutely concentrated in the financial services sector in the City of London which had to be quickly deregulated, opened up and globalised as the same technology revolutionised the entire industry worldwide. The third reason was the increasing strength and self confidence of the British economy. The fourth was the growth in importance of new kinds of global high-tech enterprises with very specific expectations and demands. Yet another and very far reaching reason was the modernising consequences of the privatisation of a very large and hitherto somewhat inert part of the UK economy – previously state controlled and nationalised industries. Several of Bennetts Associates' corporate buildings have been for clients of this kind – PowerGen, British Telecom and Wessex Water. Some of these pressures for change listed above were, of course, worldwide while others, and perhaps the most significant, are quite specific to the British economy.

All these factors working together resulted in a rapid turnaround in office design leading by the mid-1980s to a number of pioneering and very high quality British office buildings, some for corporate clients, others for developers. Examples of the former are Norman Foster's Willis Faber Dumas building in Ipswich, Arup Associates' Gateway 2 headquarters for Wiggins Teape in Basingstoke, and Richard Rogers' Corporation of Lloyds building in the City of London. Examples of the latter are Norman Foster's ITN Building in Holborn, Arup Associates' 1 Finsbury Avenue and earlier phases of Broadgate, both in the City of London, as well as their joint masterplanning with DEGW of Stockley Park near Heathrow.

Architecturally these projects, although they vary greatly, can be distinguished from their predecessors by relatively adventurous space planning features such as strategically located atria, big, simple contiguous floor plates, much more attention given to the design of circulation spaces, rationally designed cores, as well as superior levels of servicing made possible, for example, by tightly zoned air-conditioning and access floors. These projects are also distinguished by imaginative brief writing and by meticulous detailing and construction. That they are all memorably handsome in architectural terms should not be taken for granted given the low design standard of their undistinguished predecessors.

What this new generation of British office buildings amply demonstrates is:

– the growing interest among many British architects in thinking fundamentally and innovatively about fast, economic, environmentally sustainable forms of construction;
– the willingness of certain developers, most notably Stuart Lipton of Stanhope, later to be Chairman of the Commission for Architecture and the Built Environment (CABE), to procure the best architectural talent;
– an entirely new willingness of British architects to work as co-workers, in effect, within integrated design and production teams, alongside developers, contractors and engineers;
– an unprecedented acceptance of the division of labour between the design of the architectural shell and the office interior.
– a new respect for brief writing and the strong influence on office design and delivery of systematic user research largely stimulated by the unexpected challenges of new forms of Information Technology;

**Wessex Water
Operations Centre**
Left: The stepped
volumes of the building
follow the contours of
the landscape

Offices for corporate clients: comparative analysis of floor plans
From left: PowerGen Headquarters, Coventry; John Menzies, Edinburgh Park; BT, Edinburgh Park; Wessex Water Operations Centre, Bath; Sophos Headquarters, Abingdon

In all cases north is to the top

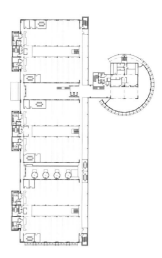

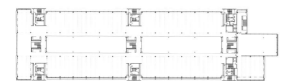 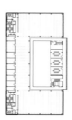

In other words UK architects had at long last learned the essential rules of office development that had been hammered out one hundred years before in the US. And, of course, before very long some of the very best American architectural practices began to do excellent work in the UK, often of a higher architectural standard than the same firms were able to achieve in their increasingly cost conscious homeland.

What finally died in this sea change was the long held British architectural belief based on a curious mixture of Arts and Crafts ideology and Modernist theory that all buildings, including office buildings, should be autonomously shaped by the unifying vision of the architect and should be the architect's unique and total responsibility.

The rediscovery of the office building

The stimulus provided in the early 1990s by the changed climate described above, which is so easy to explain today but which seemed inconclusive and confusing at the time, has turned out to be hugely important to Bennetts Associates' considerable subsequent contributions to office design in their newly founded practice. It is significant that Rab Bennetts himself before the founding of Bennetts Associates, had worked on several of the key Arup Associates projects mentioned above and that he was deeply involved in and heavily influenced by the philosophical debates that these changes stimulated.

Essentially what had happened was that communication had been opened up between two formerly irreconcilable architectural positions: the first of which is that the architect's vision is unique and all embracing and the second of which is that the design of such complex and time dependant entities as office buildings is an inherently collaborative, interdisciplinary and scientific enterprise. Both positions have always had a great deal to be said for them. The idea that both could be reconciled operationally in the context of commercial practice was completely new. If at this moment the future Bennetts Associates' had glimpsed the golden bough amid the dark and tumbling foliage, what followed next certainly depended upon demonstrable and consistent intelligence, agility, decisiveness, and imagination – not to mention sheer persistence and perseverance.

The fundamental lesson is surely that in office design architects

don't have to abandon their design principles in order to respond imaginatively to user interests.

Nothing remotely similar, nothing on the same scale or with the same completeness, has happened in the last two decades to office architecture and interior design within the US. Rather the opposite in fact; because of extraordinary cost cutting pressures within the already highly routinised and formulaic American office design delivery process office standards have, if anything, declined. Innovation is almost impossible to justify to developers except in terms of driving down costs. Meanwhile office design in Britain benefited from the crisis of the early 1980s because it was quickly obvious to everyone seriously involved in office development and office design that in order to survive economically something new and different and better had to be done. It is also true that US office buildings which had up to that time been far more advanced were able to absorb the first shocks of new Information Technology in the 1980s, largely through better facilities management rather than the revision of design standards. Moreover for political and economic reasons the challenges of worker participation in the design process have had little impact upon office developers or corporate clients. Nor, with very few exceptions, has the challenge of sustainability been addressed in an economy addicted to cheap energy. Consequently compared to 25 years ago British office design has shot ahead and is now generally more advanced than even the best American practice.

And, of course, Bennetts Associates has played a leading part throughout. The practice learned early from North American office design processes that specialist disciplines are not a threat but are instead a powerful means of enhancing design overall. Equally importantly Bennetts Associates learned from European office development that a wider and richer typology of office design is available that includes building forms based on the linear atrium or 'street' as well as on distinctly separate 'pavilions' (like PowerGen and Wessex Water in which floor plates are separated by light wells or atria and linked by generous circulation). What both 'street' and 'pavilion' office types have in common is that generous circulation is given the importance it deserves not just as an architectural gesture but much more practically to support businesses which increasingly

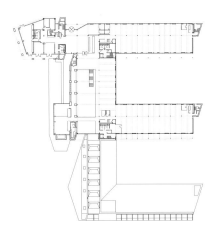

depend upon transparency, accessibility and knowledge based discourse to stimulate the constant social interaction they need to operate successfully.

Offices for corporate clients

What Bennetts Associates has done so successfully is to graft the superb craftsmanship of its architectural convictions on to a much more subtle, enquiring, intellectual approach to understanding the changing requirements of both developers and corporate office users. The practice has not been afraid to learn from international experience and has been eager to co-operate with the new specialisms, skills and research initiatives which have developed in office design in the UK since the early 1980s. This approach is what makes the line of development in their office work so coherent and consistent.

The Wiggins Teape headquarters in Basingstoke, designed by Arup Associates in the mid-1980s, with Rab Bennetts as a member of the design team, is one of the first examples of what in retrospect can be clearly seen to be a new generation of British office buildings. While Bennetts Associates has taken the essential ideas latent in that prototype as far forward as any other practice the following distinctive features still stand out in all the practice's office projects:

– the emphasis on and extreme clarity of entry and of vertical and
  horizontal circulation;
– the skilful exploitation of the atrium (or atria) not just as a means
  of playing with light but as a powerful expression of corporate
  transparency and unity;
– reliance on the open plan to provide a collaborative
  working environment;
– imaginative location and design of meeting and social spaces
– the office as a communicative device;
– the rigorous way in which each building has been treated as
  an integrated environmental system;
– the rationality and consistency with which each building has
  been designed and fabricated, nothing superfluous, nothing false.

The development of the last two ideas – sustainability and rationality – has been the most striking. Both are closely related to the priorities of

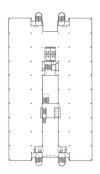

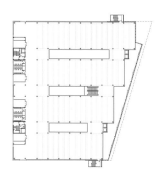

both corporate and developer clients. What Bennetts Associates has made out of the architecture of the office, both exteriors and interiors, is an aesthetic based on honesty, consistency and economy of means.

– PowerGen Headquarters, Coventry, 1994
– John Menzies Edinburgh Park, Edinburgh, 1995
– BT Edinburgh Park, Edinburgh, 1999
– Wessex Water Operations Centre, Bath, 2001
– Sophos Headquarters, Oxfordshire, 2003.

Offices for developers

Equal rigour and consistency are apparent in Bennetts Associates' work for office developers – not the easiest of clients especially when they are working within the tight margins considered appropriate for office buildings on out of town sites and business parks. Other architects designing such offices have been content to coast along on the achievements and the reforms of the 1980s, not always avoiding a certain entropy. There are far too many steel framed office factories with interiors that have no particular connection with arbitrary, flashy exteriors. Bennetts Associates in contrast has succeeded in creating its own programme of continuous improvement of the speculative office building as a product.

– Reading Office Development, Berkshire, for Speyhawk, 1989
– Heathrow World Business Centre, London, for BAA,
  commenced construction 1996
– Devonshire Square Offices, London, for AXA, 2002
– New Street Square, London EC4, for Land Securities,
  2003 – (under construction)
– City Place Offices, Gatwick, for BAA, 2003
– University Departments for Edinburgh University, 2003 –

While the first three of these projects have suspended ceilings and somewhat conventional air-conditioning systems, a consistent link between exterior and interior is achieved through massing and through a variety of environmental controls designed into the building skin. On the last two projects Bennetts Associates has been allowed to go much further by introducing internal exposed structures as a way of

further controlling the environment and reinforcing the continuity and the integrity of the connection between outside and inside. Environmental engineering is simply one more weapon in achieving a consistent, rigorous and intellectually rewarding architecture.

All the projects listed above, whether for corporate clients or for developers (including a university), demonstrate the sheer professionalism of Bennetts Associates' design process. Briefing is carefully done – and not only for corporate clients. Bennetts Associates' brief for the New Street Square development, for example, is a model of its kind. Nothing is left to chance. Everything has a reason. Interiors complement exteriors. Each building not only works but the practice always makes why the project works manifest. Devonshire Square, for example, is an exceptionally honest and consistent piece of design on a demanding site for a cost conscious developer. Such architectural rigour and honesty are still rare even in the very best British developments.

The as yet uncompleted New Street Square project represents a major change of scale in the Bennetts Associates' project portfolio – a high rise, dense, mixed-use project which is intended to complement and clarify the complex, many layered fabric of the City of London without any compromise or the faintest hint of pastiche creating a new kind of urban place with a special character of its own. Potterrow in Edinburgh, while strictly speaking a university building rather than a speculative office development, exhibits the same understanding of changing patterns of use while simultaneously creating a real sense of urban place.

Conflicts and resolutions

For a relatively young practice to have achieved such an impressive body of work on one building type is by any standards an impressive achievement and demonstrates considerable maturity. It also demonstrates the power of Bennetts Associates' processes; conflicts have occurred frequently in the creation of this outstanding portfolio of office projects for both corporate clients and developers but they have all been addressed. They include such generic and challenging matters as:

– Reconciling developers' financial goals with tenants' interests
– Designing simultaneously for long term and short term design horizons

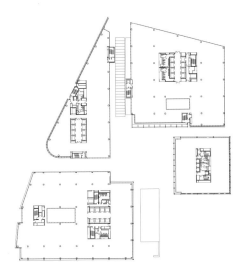

- Dealing with mixed, changing and unpredictable patterns of use
- Finding an interior design language that is robust enough to be taken as seriously in its own right as the practice's splendidly spare architecture
- Balancing the provision of internal staff amenities while creating self evidently useful external places and landscaping
- Supplementing the business logic of business parks with wider and more subtle urban qualities.

These are classically intractable issues. But to Bennetts Associates, given their highly intelligent design and briefing process, they are all grist to the mill. The practice is at its best when it is dealing with the awkward and the problematic. These architects like transforming the difficult into the extraordinary. Occasionally the golden bough may have had to be wrenched a little more roughly than usual from the tree but the effort, as demonstrated by the projects illustrated in this essay, has always been worthwhile. What is best about Bennetts Associates is that it always takes the high ground. The practice's highly moral approach to architecture is as concerned about overcoming ethical and political untidiness as about resolving each detail, each piece of space planning, each urbanistic episode in the most direct and honest way. Disguising difficulties of any kind is abhorrent. The simultaneous quest for rock like authenticity in both ethics and design sense will set the agenda for the next decades of the practice's work. The criteria by which the success of the practice will ultimately be judged embrace real world issues and transcend the somewhat limited and internalised design ambitions with which the Arts and Crafts and Modern Movement architects were too easily satisfied.

Into the future
Bennetts Associates has thrived on real time encounters in real life situations with tough business enterprises, corporate clients and developers, many of whom have never before had unrestricted access to the high levels of talent, intelligence, energy and imagination of first class architects who care deeply for client and user interests. Such clients are lucky to have access to architects who worry about the interiors of office buildings as much as the exteriors, and who are very

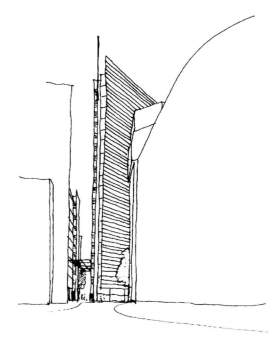

knowledgeable about how well offices can work for users and clients. In office design business criteria operate at a number of levels, not just how efficient office buildings are but also how effective, i.e. what value their buildings add to work processes, as well as how expressive, i.e. the eloquence and force with which buildings broadcast appropriate and consistent messages internally and externally. Bennetts Associates understands these criteria. The practice also cares deeply about how well its buildings are made, what they contribute to the urban environment and how little damage they wreak on our vulnerable environment.

Bennetts Associates has been lucky that the UK for the last two decades has been a very fertile place for architects working on office design. They are equally fortunate that they are not alone. They have in the UK the benefit of being part of a generation of highly talented and energetic architectural competitors working in similar fields with similarly demanding clients: Norman Foster, Richard Rogers and Ted Cullinan were pioneers. Michael Hopkins and Nicholas Grimshaw are in the next cohort followed by other talented practices including Allies and Morrison, John McAslan and Fletcher Priest. These architects working in office design in the last two or three decades in the UK have been challenged in the right way at the right time and have risen magnificently to the occasion.

There is no reason to expect this hard won advantage to continue indefinitely. American architects, inherently no less talented than their British counterparts, especially given the resources of their much larger, more dynamic and consistently more successful economy, may well recover their poise. Northern European office architects have a much richer and more sophisticated social democratic tradition to draw upon as well as an even stronger interest in environmental quality. More importantly the office building must now be regarded as a particularly unstable building type. Being excellent at designing the offices of one decade, as both the Americans and the Northern Europeans have found, may turn into a curse in the next.

The challenge to architects in office design today is enormous,

much more difficult than in the early 1980s. The advent of robust, reliable, ubiquitous information technology changes everything. Distributed ways of working are already rapidly eroding design conventions that have worked for decades, even centuries. Emerging patterns of office work are more mobile, more fluid, more agile. Virtual office work is already challenging real work done in real places in real time. The design of physical office buildings will soon be overtaken by the necessity to pay at least as much attention to the design of regionally and globally distributed networks as to individual office buildings. New technologies, new business structures, new conventions in the use of space and time mean that office architects of Bennetts Associates' generation will inevitably have to address the radical reinvention of the workplace, the office building and the city.

To convey some idea of the architectural potential of the growing importance of virtuality in office design it may help to use a strong image. Imagine a virtual world on another planet in which a virtual being, a genius among his or her kind, despite enjoying the many conveniences of virtuality, lights upon the totally novel idea of *place*. What kinds of argument would such a being have to use to convince his or her fellow beings to adopt the alien, heretical and disturbing notion of place? Such arguments would certainly embrace sociability, connectedness, serendipity, memory, associations, metaphor, non-linearity, particularity, all the qualities that endow cities and spaces with meaning. From this perspective place will certainly become more rather than less important.

Bennetts Associates, of course, will rise to this challenge as briskly, efficiently and intelligently as it has to every other challenge it has ever had to face. The practice's own old/new office which lies on the borders of bricky Islington and creative Clerkenwell, with its precious mixture of rationality and serendipity, of advanced technology and old fashioned courtesy, of the given and the stylish, of modesty and artistry, of wide ranging interests and a strong sense of place is a microcosm of Bennetts Associates' huge imaginative potential as creative designers of new kinds of places for working at every scale.

PROJECTS G–O

Guildford Civic Hall Competition, Surrey

Hampstead Theatre, London

Heathrow Airport Visitor Centre, London

Heathrow World Business Centre, London

John Menzies Edinburgh Park, Edinburgh

Loch Lomond Gateway and Orientation
Centre, West Dunbartonshire

Medicentre, Inverness

Mark Lane Offices, City of London

Museum of the Moving Image, London

New Street Square, City of London

Olympic Aquatics Centre Competition, London

GUILDFORD CIVIC HALL COMPETITION SURREY, 2004–

Guildford's Civic Hall is to be redeveloped as a major new arts venue for the people of Guildford and south east England. Bennetts Associates' competition-winning scheme reorientates the building so that the main entrance addresses the historic thoroughfare of Guildford High Street. The glazed foyer engages with the topography of the site and an area of protected parkland, resulting in a series of contrasting spaces that screen the main volume of the hall. The auditorium, which has a variable capacity of 1,200 seated and 2,000 standing, is capable of adaptation from orchestral to amplified musical events, as well as other uses. The simple rectangular volume of the auditorium creates a flexible civic space which has an optimum proportion for acoustics.

The orientation of the stage towards the main entrance heightens the entry sequence and allows all back-of-house facilities to be concealed below a new public square. Other facilities include a flexible studio theatre and function suite. The overall scheme also includes large residential components which provide the majority of the funding for the Civic Hall.

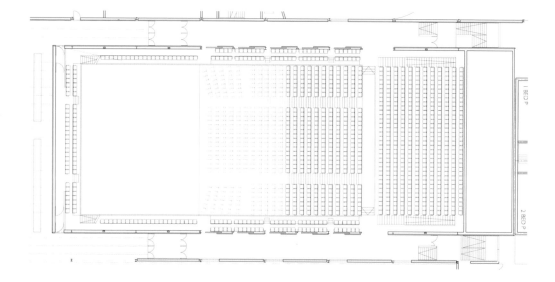

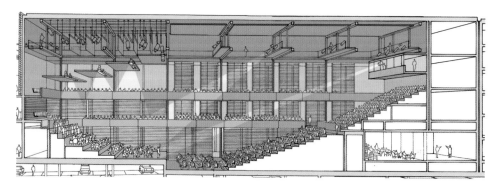

Guildford Civic Hall Competition
Left, above: Plan

Left, below: Section, arranged for a concert

Opposite, above and middle: General views of the hall and its foyers

Opposite, below: Section in context

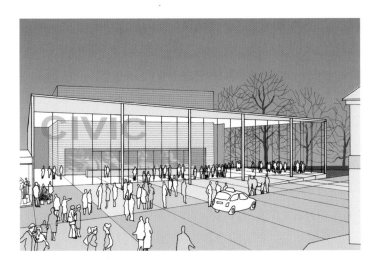

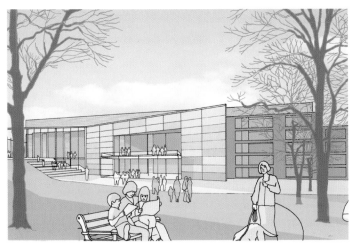

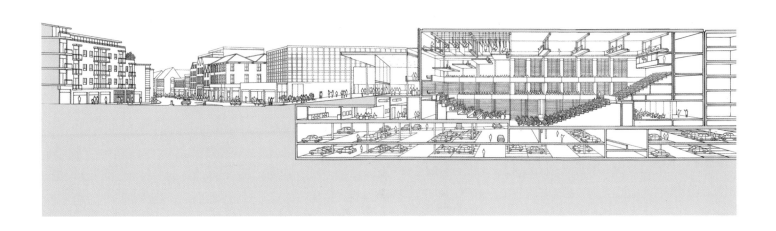

Hampstead Theatre
Above: Night view, revealing the zinc-clad auditorium and the foyer

Right: View from the new public park due to be completed in 2006

Opposite: East-west section

HAMPSTEAD THEATRE
LONDON, 1994–2003

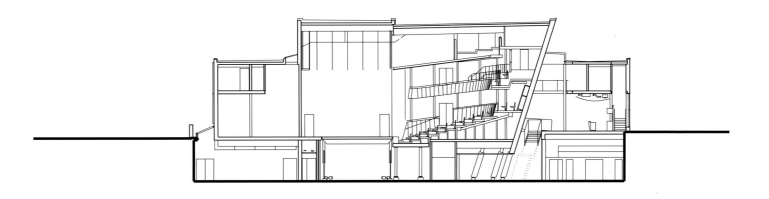

Hampstead Theatre is the first freestanding theatre to be built in London since the National Theatre in 1975. Built specifically for the purpose of producing contemporary plays, it has been designed to support Hampstead Theatre's tradition of fostering new writing, with a flexible stage and a compact auditorium that can adapt to each play and production.

Hampstead Theatre's existing home at Swiss Cottage was an enlarged Portakabin dating from the mid-1960s. As the new theatre was to be significantly larger, Bennetts Associates initiated a masterplan for the whole Swiss Cottage block, not only to find a more appropriate site but also in response to the area's run-down condition. The masterplan subsequently became the vehicle for major regeneration, implemented by Camden Council as landowner, with the theatre as the catalyst.

The building is conceived as a simple, rectangular pavilion in the setting of an urban park, with two floors above ground and one below. Volumetrically, the auditorium adopts the form of a sloping cylinder, rising from deep within the building and thrusting through the roof. The complex space between the curves of the auditorium and the straight lines of the enclosing pavilion provides a dynamic setting for the audience as it gathers before the performance, and for interval drinks. The angular bridges that cross the void accentuate the sense of anticipation before entering the auditorium.

Although the auditorium has considerable flexibility in its staging arrangements, it is intended at all times to be a complete room – the antithesis of the 'black-box' theatre. With a maximum audience approaching double that of the previous building, the adoption of an elliptical layout means that

the rear stalls are as close to the stage, maintaining the same sense of intimacy whilst avoiding direct comparisons with the shoebox like interior of the Portakabin.

An education room and rehearsal room are located in the basement, which also incorporates a vehicle ramp to the adjacent office block.

The project has taken nine years from inception to completion, with extended periods in the planning, public consultation and funding stages while alternative schemes were explored and agreements with adjoining properties finalised.

Hampstead Theatre
Top: Detail of the
auditorium

Above: An early model

Right (from top): First;
ground; and basement
floor plans

Opposite, above: The
auditorium in coventional
stage format

Opposite, below: Detail
of stalls and circle

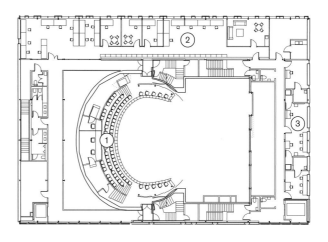

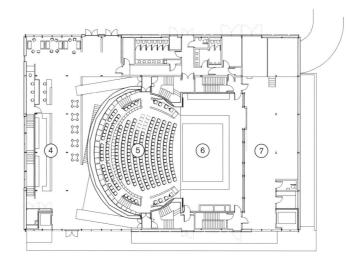

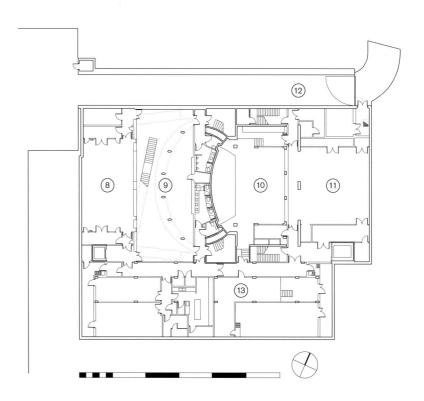

Key
1 Circle
2 Administration
3 Dressing rooms
4 Bar/foyer
5 Stalls
6 Stage
(proscenium layout)
7 Workshop
8 Education room
9 Lower
foyer/boardroom
10 Under-stage area
11 Rehearsal room
12 Car access to
office block
13 Plantrooms

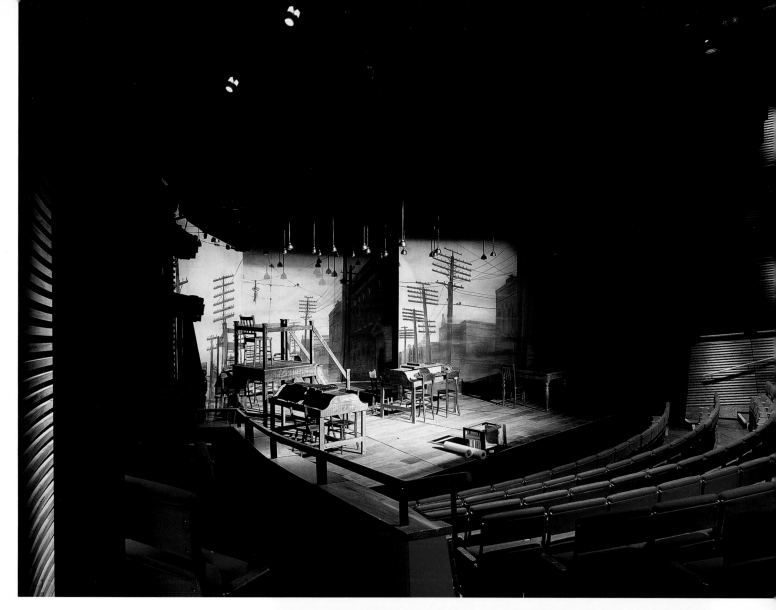

Hampstead Theatre

Above: The steel
structure illustrates
the complexity of the
auditorium geometry

Top, left and right:
Bridges to the auditorium
from the foyer

Right: The foyer and
bar, showing Martin
Richman's lighting panels

Opposite: Facade detail

HEATHROW AIRPORT VISITOR CENTRE
LONDON, 1994–95

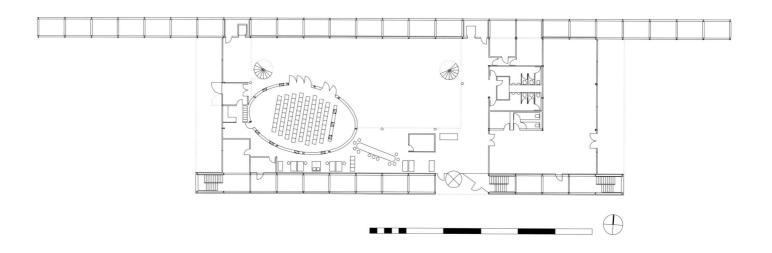

The identity of this modest sized building owes much to its simplicity in plan and the speed of its design and construction.

Following a brief design competition, the Heathrow Airport Visitor Centre was designed and built in only nine months, immediately prior to the 1995 Public Inquiry into the Terminal 5 Development. Although the building's primary function is a major exhibition about the workings of the airport, it also contains a public information point, a job centre and a small auditorium. As the building is located directly beside Heathrow's north runway, a cafe on the upper level serves as a popular viewing gallery for plane spotters.

The simplicity of the design concept was essential to completing the project on time. Two parallel walls, fabricated from identical steel frames regardless of load, simply support an inverted, curved roof structure. The north wall has largely solid cladding and is covered with climbing plants, aided by a galvanised grillage that extends beyond the building to the perimeter of the site in order to enhance the building's apparent scale. The south wall is clad in two layers of frameless glazing bolted directly to the steel frame so as to avoid long-delivery curtain walling, forming an effective two metre wide barrier to aircraft noise whilst retaining complete transparency. The width of the cavity is also used to accommodate escape stairs, solar shading and cleaning apparatus.

The Heathrow Airport Visitor Centre was Bennetts Associates' second major commission for BAA (formerly British Airports Authority) and was followed by the World Business Centre on the adjacent site.

**Heathrow Airport
Visitor Centre**
Above: View from
the Bath Road in 1995.
Climbing plants now
cover the galvanised
mesh

Right: The simplicity of
the steel frame allowed
rapid construction

Left: Ground floor plan.
The exhibition space and
lecture room is to the left
of the entrance, the job
centre is on the right

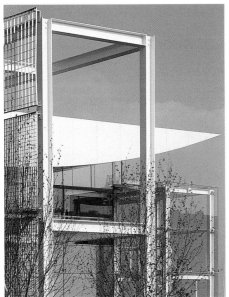

**Heathrow Airport
Visitor Centre**
Above: View from
the runway

Left: Frameless glazing
bolted to the steel
structure

Far left: Steel frame detail

Opposite: Unobstructed
views of the runway
through the glazed
cavity wall

Heathrow World Business Centre

Above: Entrance elevation facing south towards the runway

Right: Site plan, with the Visitor Centre to the left of the four pavilions. All buildings are set back from the runway to clear height restraints

Opposite: View from the central terminal complex. As at 2005, three pavilions have been constructed; the fourth is a computer montage

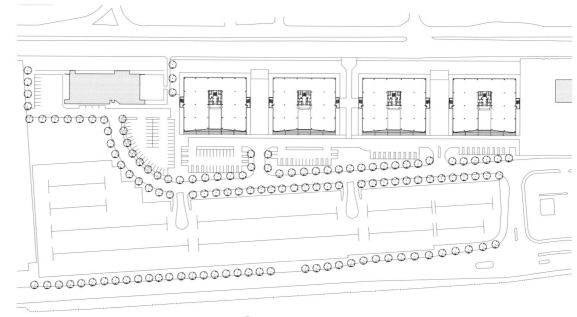

HEATHROW WORLD BUSINESS CENTRE
LONDON, 1995–

Four virtually identical office buildings give the impression of a continuous group, directly addressing the heroic scale of Heathrow Airport's north runway. The development is analogous to a Georgian terrace, where individual identity is subordinate to the whole, in an attempt to introduce a sense of order to the visual chaos of the airport's surroundings.

The buildings are aimed at airport-related companies, with up to four different tenants per floor. The central core and perimeter stairs allow easy subdivision of the space and the potential for future links between buildings. The placement of an atrium in front of each main core allows maximum visibility, both for the occupants deep within the

building and for the millions of passengers who will see the development at speed from the runway. The use of a strong colour on each core, ranging from red in phase one to jade, ochre and navy blue in phase four, reflects the need for a simple, graphic device that can be registered at 320 kilometres per hour.

Full-height glazing on the south facade exploits the spectacular views of planes taking off and landing, with large, wide-spaced louvres dealing with excessive solar gain. The centre of the south facade is indented to signify the main entrance.

The project also addresses the client's commitment to radical reform of the

construction industry through lower costs, prefabricated building techniques and higher levels of productivity, becoming an exemplar for BAA's Chief Executive, Sir John Egan following his 1998 report "Rethinking Construction".

Subsequently, the project became known as the BAA Standard Office Product and was used in modified form by other architects and contractors at various UK airports. For Bennetts Associates, these later examples tended to illustrate that standard components can be successful, but that standard buildings are unlikely to offer sufficient response to context.

Heathrow World Business Centre

Top: View of office floor

Above, left: Rear elevation to the Bath Road. The earlier Visitor Centre is beyond

Above, right: View across office floor to the north runway

Right: Typical floor plan, which is subdivisible into four separate tenancies

Opposite: Atrium and core of the first pavilion

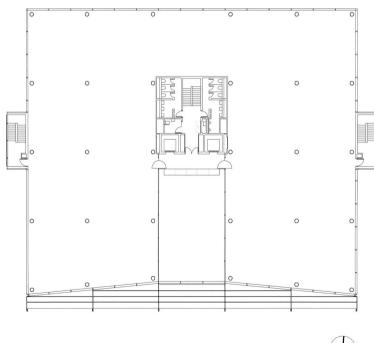

JOHN MENZIES EDINBURGH PARK
EDINBURGH, 1993–95

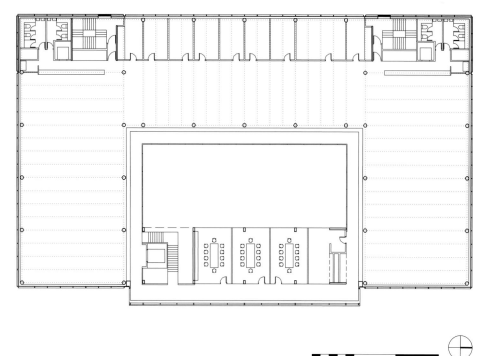

Inspired by the unity of Georgian Edinburgh, Richard Meier's masterplan for Edinburgh Park envisages all but the most prominent sites being developed in a cohesive way, with a consistency of scale, alignment and materials that complements the park's exceptional landscape. As the first site to be developed within the principal range of buildings, the John Menzies headquarters represented the first test of the masterplan guidelines and established a precedent for the quality of subsequent developments.

The plan takes the form of a quadrangle, approached like a country house in a way that conceals the view until the building has been entered. A sequence of internal spaces aids the transition from the point of arrival through the central hall and a waterside pavilion to the landscape. The sense of directionality is reinforced by repetitive office floorplates on three sides and a narrower block of accommodation on the fourth. This transparent band of accommodation and the circulation route that links it to the main office areas enable all the occupants to see the best views to the south and east and is the location for communal meeting rooms, the restaurant and the boardrooms.

With relatively narrow floorplates, good levels of daylight and high thermal mass, the building develops the same principles of a pleasant, energy efficient workplace as the PowerGen project, which was under construction at the time John Menzies was designed. However, analysis of the more northerly climatic conditions, such as sun angles, wind speeds and temperatures, led to significant differences in the detailed design and, whilst there are opening windows around the perimeter, the use of displacement ventilation provides a more energy-efficient alternative to natural ventilation.

As with its predecessor, the exposed structure expresses the integrity of the architecture, defining the internal space and its ineradicable relationship to the building's engineering functions.

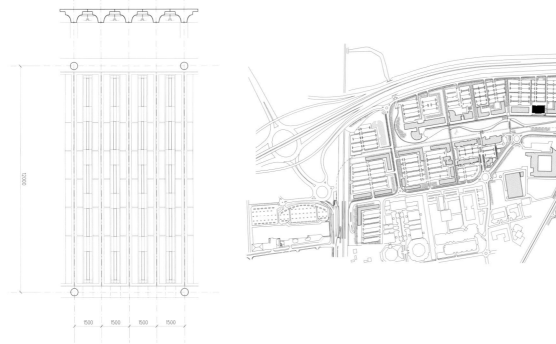

1500 1500 1500 1500

**John Menzies
Edinburgh Park**
Above: General views
of the office and atrium
areas. As with many other
buildings by Bennetts
Associates, the structure
defines the quality of its
major and minor spaces

Opposite: The east
elevation before
construction of
neighbouring buildings

Loch Lomond Gateway and Orientation Centre
Above: The woodland facade

Right: The transparency of the building emphasises the landscape

Opposite: Site plan

LOCH LOMOND GATEWAY
AND ORIENTATION CENTRE
WEST DUNBARTONSHIRE, 1999–2002

Located at the southern tip of Loch Lomond not far from Glasgow, this steel pavilion is a metaphor for the decline of local industry and its replacement by tourism. It also acts as a threshold to the newly designated National Park.

Loch Lomond and the Trossachs National Park required a visitor facility that could cope with millions of visitors per year whilst introducing the concept of sustainability in the natural environment. As the smallest of three buildings that together make up the Lomond Shores development, the centre acts as a symbolic gateway to the woodlands along the shore beyond the development and, hence, to the National Park itself. In contrast to many other visitor centres, the transparency of its construction suggests

that the main exhibit is the world outside and, in sympathy with the building, the exhibition design comprises a number of simple cubes that are positioned well clear of the external walls. To accentuate the relationship with the landscape, the last structural bay of the building is open-sided and cantilevers over the water.

A 100-metre long, freestanding, timber colonnade reinforces the idea of a threshold between the centre and the development as a whole, as a way of distinguishing the smallest building's role from that of its more commercial neighbours and ensuring a significance to visitors beyond its modest size. The entrance lobby and main stair landing form a prominent part of the colonnade's function and visual composition.

Although the original concept of using salvaged steel from a disused industrial building for the structure was not adopted, the building reduces its environmental impacts in several ways through minimal servicing and use of low carbon materials wherever appropriate. For example, the timber colonnade is fabricated from storm-damaged oak donated by the French Government. The site itself is a reclaimed gravel pit, a legacy from the industrial heyday of the nearby Clyde and Leven Valleys.

The project includes reinvigorating the previously neglected landscape of the adjacent promontory, adding boardwalks above marshy ground, and an extensive series of public art installations.

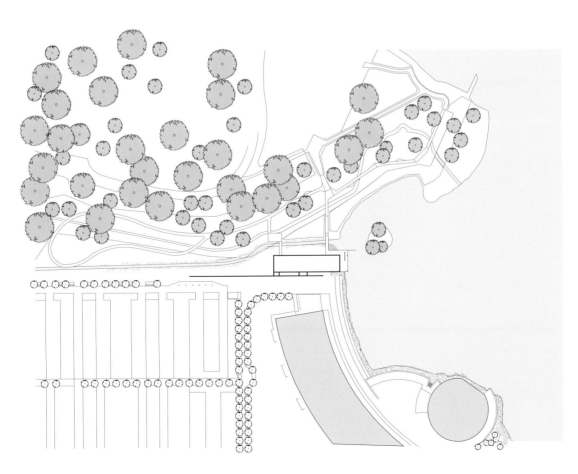

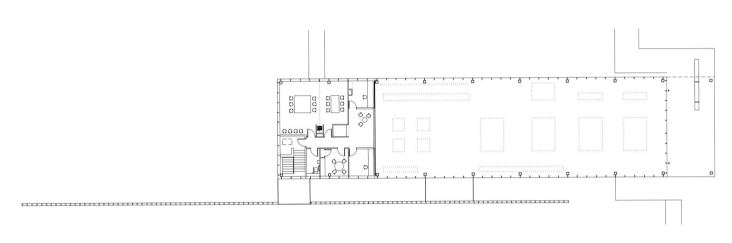

Loch Lomond Gateway and Orientation Centre

Top, left: The entrance facade

Top, right: The entrance lobby, between the oak colonnade and the glazed pavilion

Above: Upper floor plan

Left: The pavilion seen from the lake

Opposite: The structure projects over the loch

**Loch Lomond Gateway
and Orientation Centre**
Above: The entrance to
the pavilion

Above, left: The exhibition
installation

Right: The projecting
structural bay marks
the beginning of the
boardwalk to the
woodland

Opposite, above:
Entrance elevation,
showing the colonnade

Opposite, below: Artificial
light reveals the timber
ceiling and the exhibition
elements at dusk

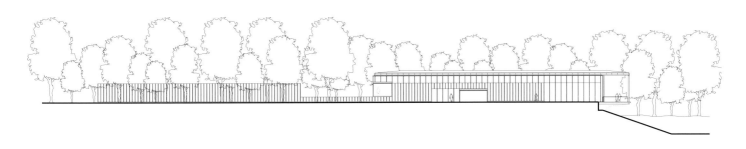

MEDICENTRE
INVERNESS, 2003 –

This centre for interdisciplinary healthcare education is located in the grounds of Raigmore Hospital, Inverness, in the north of Scotland. It caters for a wide range of accommodation, including clinical skills teaching, offices, dentistry, light laboratories, incubators and research for both the National Health Service and two universities. The Medicentre also incorporates shared lecture theatres, a library, IT support and a cafe.

The building takes the form of a courtyard and is to be built in two L-shaped phases, with the shared accommodation connected by a double-height hall close to the main entrance. This space is intended to bring all the disparate users together to strengthen the building's interdisciplinary purpose. The height of the building is strictly limited by the proximity of a nearby helicopter landing area.

The form of construction adopts a similar pattern to other low-energy buildings by Bennetts Associates, with an exposed structure, suspended light assemblies and natural ventilation. Initial studies for vaulted, pre-cast concrete slabs revealed supply difficulties in this part of the UK, so a carefully detailed steel frame and in situ flat slab has been adopted throughout. External cladding is a combination of curtain walling and terracotta panels, with extensive sunshading to the largest glazed surfaces. The terracotta is used to frame the elevations and give the building a degree of visual impact compared to nearby hospital facilities. The main conference/lecture facility is expressed as a separate, copper-clad volume and provides an 'anchor' adjacent to the main entrance.

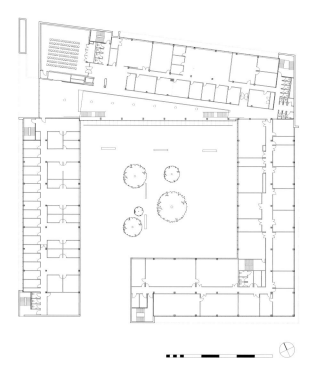

Medicentre
Above: Masterplan

Above, right: Upper floor plan

Opposite, above: Perspective from the north. Cladding to the lecture theatre is copper

Opposite, below: The approach to the entrance. Elevations are visually framed in terracotta cladding

Mark Lane Offices

Above: Computer montage from Tower Bridge, showing the building in front of 30 St Mary Axe

Right: Views of model

Opposite, top: Site plan

Opposite, below left: Upper floor plan, with conservatory garden

Opposite, below right: Cross section

MARK LANE OFFICES
CITY OF LONDON, 2001–

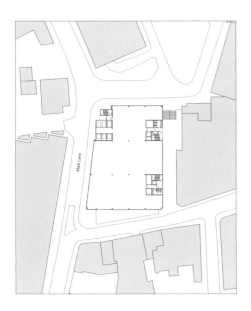

This scheme uses the angular language of conservatories and solar control as the vehicle for punctuating the skyline when viewed from the northern bastion of Tower Bridge – a point considered by the City planners critical to the setting of the Tower of London – and for inserting a relatively tall building at the edge of a conservation area.

The site occupies a small city block close to Fenchurch Street Station, at the point where modest-scale buildings give way to structures of ten to 20 floors. As a way of making the transition between these two scales, the proposed development has 15 floors to the north and nine floors to the south, with a stepped profile that is unified by a sloping canopy. The spaces beneath the canopy take the form of atrium-scale conservatories

accessed from the upper office floors, with spectacular views towards the Tower of London, Tower Bridge and the Thames. To prevent excessive solar gain, large louvres keep direct sunlight off the sloping glazed surfaces. It is intended that these louvres will take the form of photovoltaic panels.

The internal layout of the 15,000 square metre building places two cores on the east side, where the view is restricted by the adjoining building, with a minimum number of columns in the general office space. At street level, the main entrance is on the west side from Mark Lane, with glazed lifts occupying the corner facing Fenchurch Street at the point where the alignment of Mark Lane changes direction. Planning consent was obtained in 2002.

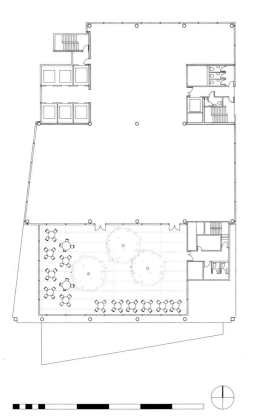

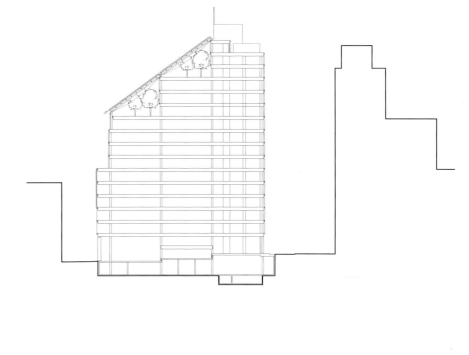

MUSEUM OF THE MOVING IMAGE
LONDON, 1997

Legibility and identity were critical to this Lottery-funded proposal, injecting a notoriously difficult part of the South Bank complex with a clarity of circulation that turned the museum from a prescriptive to a selective experience. Bennetts Associates was already familiar with the site, having prepared designs for a new restaurant and refurbishment of the National Film Theatre (NFT) in the late 1980s.

The Museum of the Moving Image (MOMI) was created as a companion to the NFT, which had its origins in the 1951 Festival of Britain on the south bank of the Thames. The original auditorium remained under the southern abutment of Waterloo Bridge, but subsequent extensions had resulted in problems of visibility, access and operational adequacy.

The British Film Institute (BFI)'s intention was to double the size of MOMI, by moving the NFT to another site, and to create a new perception of the building as part of the South Bank reorganisation of 1997-98.

Bennetts Associates proposed adding a substantial, glazed structure to the east side of Waterloo Bridge, thereby creating an engaging new presence alongside the National Theatre. This glazed structure contained vertical and horizontal circulation, located outboard from the exhibition spaces.

The new facade rose alongside, and proud of, Waterloo Bridge and acted as a multimedia screen, with projected images revealing tantalising glimpses of the contents and activity inside. Preview displays at the threshold of each exhibition module enabled visitors to edit their experience of the museum. Tying into Richard Rogers' proposals to cover the South Bank Centre with a glass wave, Bennetts Associates' design also included a semi-public access routes crossing from the Museum to the Hayward Gallery to the west and the IMAX cinema to the east.

Although the MOMI proposals were well received by the National Lottery funding advisers and English Heritage, the Richard Rogers masterplan was abandoned in 1999 and the BFI was obliged to place their plans on hold while the future of the South Bank was resolved.

Museum of the Moving Image
Left: Site model, with the National Theatre to the left and Richard Rogers Partnership's 'Crystal Wave' to the right. MOMI is located below and alongside Waterloo Bridge

Opposite, above: The animated facade to MOMI

Opposite, below: Diagrams illustrating Waterloo Bridge, the internal spaces and the glazed circulation structure

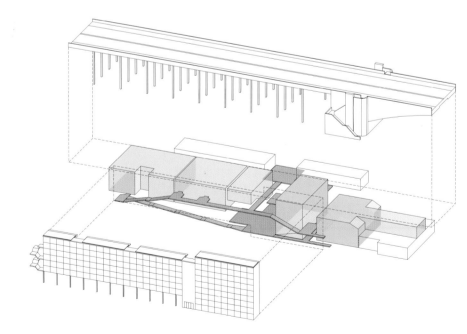

NEW STREET SQUARE
CITY OF LONDON, 2003–

The New Street Square project is one of the most significant developments in the City of London for some years, bearing comparison with Broadgate from the 1980s and Paternoster Square from the 1990s.

The intention is to create a new destination between High Holborn and Fleet Street serving the 'mid-town' area of the City, with a substantial group of new buildings set around a new public square. A tightly planned series of pedestrian routes integrates the new development with the lanes and courts that characterise the adjacent Fleet Street conservation area. These pedestrian routes converge on the new square, with cafes and shops animating the street scene alongside office entrances. A programme of public art and performance encompasses all the main spaces.

The overlaying of a regular pattern of spaces or routes with an irregular site boundary generates four plots around the square for major buildings of differing sizes and plan forms, with the intention of ensuring a degree of economic flexibility combined with the essential ingredients for a townscape with variety and drama. In addition to one high-rise tower, two medium-rise atrium buildings and one low-rise block, there is a small pavilion that serves as a management suite and access to the basement car/cycle park. Quite apart from urban design considerations, the varying height of the buildings ensures the maximum level of sunlight penetration into the square, with the tallest to the north and the lowest to the south. Scale and materiality are also used to establish appropriate relationships between the scheme and its surroundings, with the tallest being the most

assertive, its sharply pointed corner signalling the development from Holborn Circus.

By City standards, the New Street Square development is, therefore, unusually versatile and site specific but it also brings together several existing strands of thinking that have evolved over a number of previous projects by Bennetts Associates, notably sustainability and the efficient workplace. Of particular interest are the simple, adaptable floorplates, constructed in concrete without downstand beams so that there is flexibility for a variety of servicing solutions, from conventional fancoil to low-energy chilled beams. An extensive sustainability policy has been instituted on all aspects of the project from the initial brief through design, specification, demolition of the existing buildings and construction.

New Street Square
Right: Typical floor plan of the four main buildings

Far right: Site plan at ground level, showing retail and cafe spaces, loading bays, office entrances and public routes

Opposite: Computer montage of New Street Square from the south

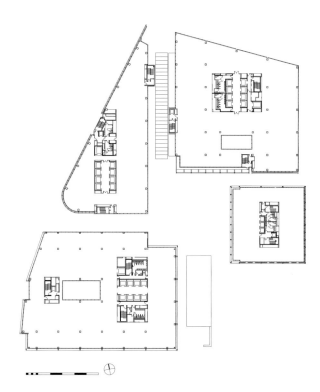

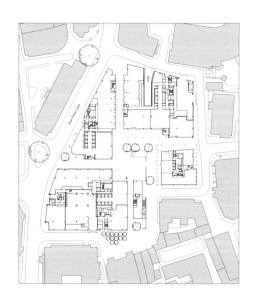

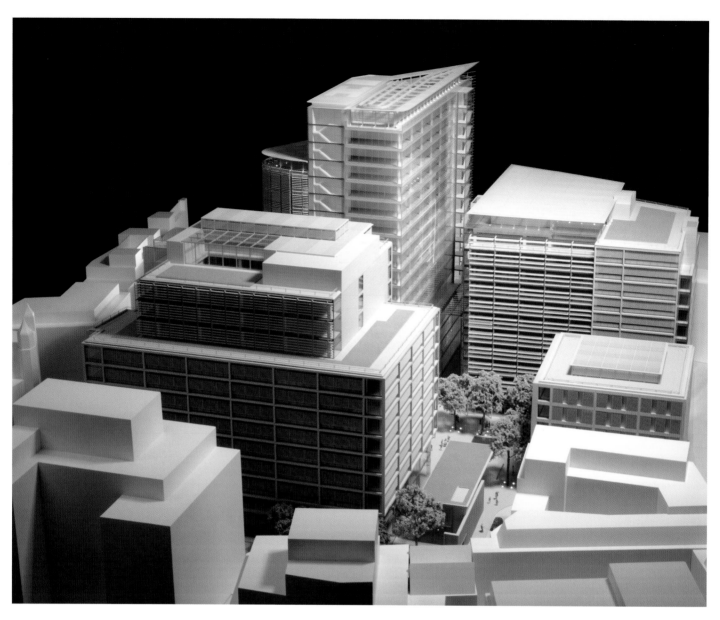

New Street Square

Above and opposite top: General views of massing model, illustrating changes of scale across the scheme

Left: Section through typical floor, showing solar shading, exposed concrete slab and chilled beam. Heavily serviced floors can accommodate conventional air conditioning within the same dimensions

Opposite, below: Computer montage view from Holborn Circus

Olympic Aquatics Centre competition
Above: The canopy of the Aquatics Centre forms the entrance to the Olympic Park and frames the view of the main stadium

Right: Site plan in legacy mode

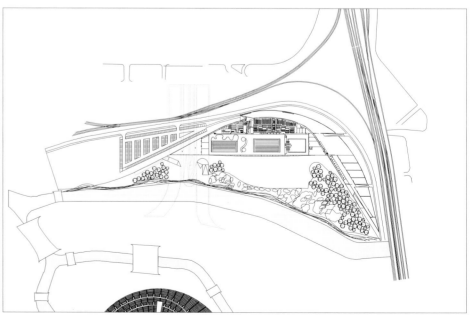

OLYMPIC AQUATICS CENTRE COMPETITION
LONDON, 2004–

London's bid for the 2012 Olympics was supported by a persuasive masterplan for regeneration of the Lea Valley as the Olympic Park and the design of some key buildings, the most developed of which was the Aquatics Centre. Bennetts Associates' proposals, made jointly with swimming specialists Studio Zoppini from Milan, used regeneration as the springboard for a highly sustainable building and landscape that would last for many years beyond the initial impact of the Games.

First, the building is placed hard up against the site's eastern boundary, so that the maximum possible land area can be devoted to external public space – a 'green piazza' that extends the long term activity from the pools area to a leisure area outside. In consequence, the building adopts a leaf-like shape, as a metaphor for the greening of the valley, which allows it to be both legible and practical in its layout.

Second, to avoid wasting resources, the huge amount of short-term Olympic event seating is accommodated and serviced by a temporary structure that can be re-used elsewhere when the Games have moved on. This means that the legacy building can be relatively compact, making it vastly more energy-efficient in the long term than would otherwise be possible. The embankment that embraces the east side of the building incorporates the combined heat and power plant for the whole complex.

Third, the entrance to the legacy building is located on the pedestrian bridge that connects the park to Stratford town centre, making it more immediately visible and accessible to future users from the local community. The entrance of the Aquatics Centre is dramatised by the roof, which sails over the pedestrian bridge to form a gateway to the Olympic complex.

Fourth, the three pools are accommodated in a single, clear-spanning volume where glazing is incorporated into the twisting shape of each major roof truss. Once the temporary Olympic seating is removed, a full-length glass wall provides visual continuity between the park and the interior.

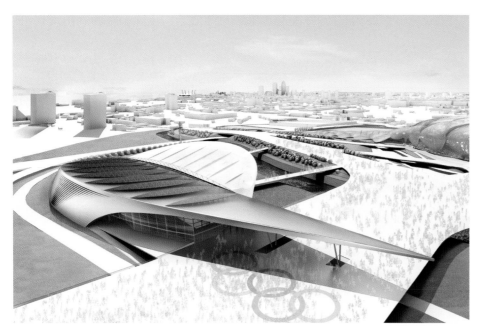

Olympic Aquatics Centre competition

Above, left: External view with Olympic temporary structures

Above, right: Internal view showing Olympic seating

Below: Plan showing temporary Olympic seating

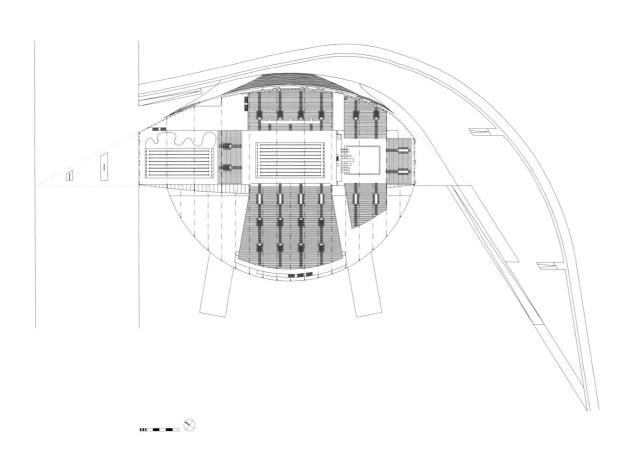

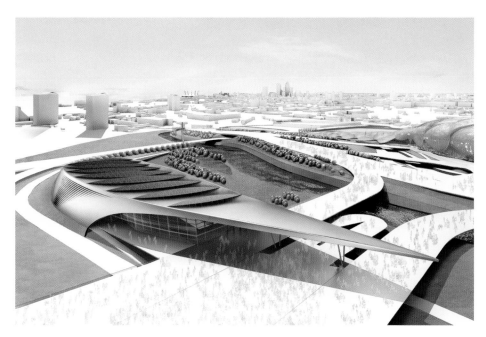

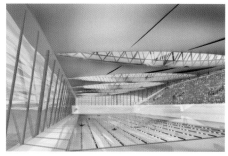

Olympic Aquatics Centre competition
Above, left: External view without Olympic temporary structures

Above, right: Internal views showing legacy format

Below: Plan showing long-term legacy format

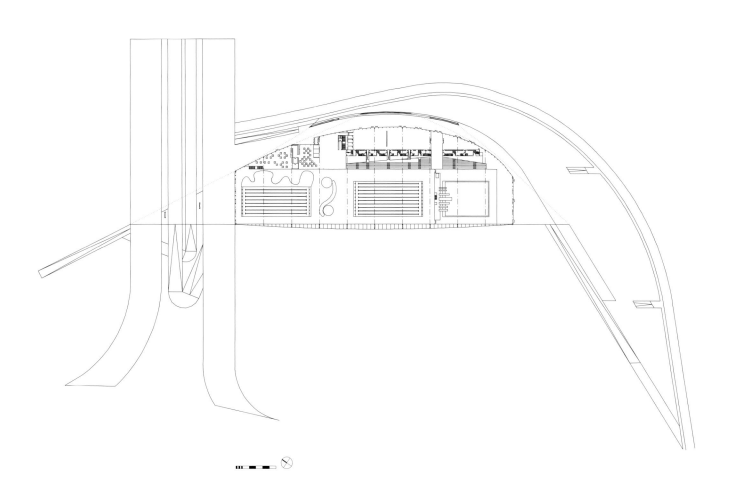

VIVIEN LOVELL
ART AND ARCHITECTURE

Art consultant Vivien Lovell identifies an approach within Bennetts Associates that embraces the work of others. Its buildings are not necessarily egocentric or iconic; the public domain is given equal attention through the design of open spaces or the inclusion of public art. The principle of collaboration is at the heart of all projects. In her commentary, Lovell traces some early influences on the practice and describes her perception of several influential projects that use public art as a vehicle for enhancement or provocation. As confidence and scale have increased, Bennetts Associates' integration of public art has addressed the public domain, as at the Westminster hotel for City Inn where an entire pedestrian street creates an unexpected destination space for London's art world. Future projects promise more surprises, but Lovell also reveals the artistic intentions of the architects themselves, through colour, light and space.

3

Loch Lomond Gateway and Orientation Centre
Opposite: *Untitled (Field of Labels)*, Vong Phaophanit

Above: The single storey steel pavilion from adjacent woodland

Introduction

A distinctive aesthetic has evolved in Bennetts Associates' architectural and public space projects over the past 18 years. It is characterised by a strong yet finessed approach to geometric and rectilinear forms, elegantly calibrated by light, shade, texture and colour. The practice has been concerned with the linking of interior and exterior spaces, and the way a building 'touches the ground', successfully locating itself in relation to its environment, for far longer than the current (and long overdue) attention being paid to the public spaces between and around buildings. This commitment to the physical environment is matched by the practice's reputation for low energy, sustainable architecture, which has been recognised in the media and by numerous awards.

Less well documented, and the focus of this essay, is the practice's distinguished track record of involving artists in their projects. As with their commitment to the public realm and sustainability, this is not based merely on current fashion, but rather on principles and sensibilities stemming from the time when Rab and Denise Bennetts were students together at Edinburgh College of Art/Heriot Watt University. The training of architecture and art students under one roof fostered acceptance of collaboration and respect for other creative disciplines, as the architect Peter Cook observed at the conference 'Context and Collaboration' held in Birmingham in 1990. He quoted the example of the Staatliche Hochschule fur Bildende Kunste – Stadelschule in Frankfurt where students commissioned each other once they had graduated. Cook also noted that collaborations between architects and artists remained harder to achieve in Britain than in any other European country. Times and attitudes have changed since then, as a result of advocacy, the desire of artists to work beyond as well as within the 'white cube' of the gallery and, not least, planning conditions that encourage the inclusion of public art. Importantly, artists and architects are, in the main, finding that working together can add richness to their own creativity. Now, it is established practice for artists to be commissioned in relation to architectural schemes, but there are few architects that can claim such a long commitment to working with artists as Bennetts Associates.

To date, over a dozen of the practice's architectural schemes and masterplans have included artists' input, from commissioning and purchasing artworks for corporate environments, to artists' installations in sound and video, to more recent collaborations with artists on architecture and public space. This is an impressive record, and constitutes a major contribution to the field known as Art and Architecture, named after the eponymous conference held at the ICA in 1982. Clearly, for art to be commissioned there has to be support from the client (and the motives will vary), but Bennetts Associates, unlike many architectural practices, will raise the issue without prompting, indicative of a curiosity and open-mindedness about the role that an artist might play in a scheme. This natural tendency for collaboration with artists (and this extends to team-working with engineers, landscape architects, planning consultants and indeed other architectural practices) arises from a desire for art within the scheme of things and a respect for the professional role and skills of artists.

The Institute of Contemporary Arts, London
Right: Jennie Moncur's floor coverings in the upper galleries

Louis Kahn
Below: The Salk Institute for Biological Studies, La Jolla, California, 1965

Richard Serra
Opposite, left: *Fulcrum*, sculpture at Broadgate, City of London, 1987

Donald Judd
Opposite, top right: *Untitled,* 1972

Finsbury Avenue, London
Opposite, below right: *White Cross Arch*, maquette for granite sculpture by Paul de Monchaux

Inevitably, in the firm's early years, some planned art projects did not happen. At Finsbury Avenue in London, there was the intention to commission the sculptor Paul de Monchaux for the public space next to a Greycoats development by Arup Associates. The proposed sculpture, an arched form in Cornish granite, would have framed beautifully the space for which it was designed, and would also have functioned as a bench. British Land acquired the site, and sadly neither artwork nor an additional building by Bennetts Associates were pursued.

What are the architectural and artistic points of reference that have informed Bennetts Associates' aesthetic? In conversation on this topic, the principals of the practice cite Louis Kahn, Arne Jacobsen (particularly St Catherine's College, Oxford), and Mies van der Rohe as early influences, although it was a trip to India in 1981 and seeing the Taj Mahal, fortified towns and palace gardens, that increased Rab's confidence to design "utterly geometric buildings and complete volumes; BT's pavilion at Edinburgh Park is, after all, a rectangle within a circle".

Brilliant manipulation of daylight characterises all of Bennetts Associates' architecture; Kahn's reference to 'structure as a giver of light' is evident in their approach. Carlo Scarpa's use of daylight and colour may also have been an influence.

These early points of reference began to inform their approach to materials, surface, space, balance, colour and light. Richard Serra's *Tilted Arc* in New York City's Federal Plaza (installed 1981, destroyed 1989) was seen on a trip to New York in the early 1980s; a few years later, the Serra sculptures installed at the first Saatchi Gallery designed

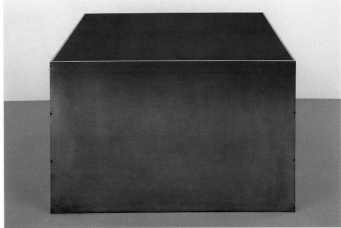

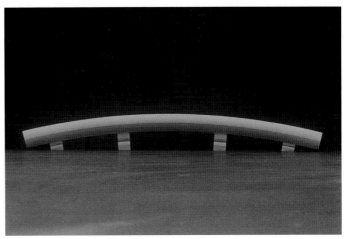

by the late Max Gordon, influenced their thinking about the spatial relationships of art to architecture in their designs for the ICA, and subsequent projects. Their admiration for Corten steel, and the firm's subsequent (thwarted) desire to incorporate it on the facade of the Devonshire Place building, must surely be inspired by Serra's habitual use of this sensuous material, as well as the Irish American architect Kevin Roche's work at the Ford Foundation in New York and elsewhere. The work of Donald Judd may also have had a subliminal influence on some aspects of the practice's thinking about volume, colour and space, for example at Brighton Central Library, which is in effect a simple geometric volume lined with a luxurious material.

Contact with art and dialogue with artists have, therefore, always stimulated the practice's creativity. At the ICA, Bennetts Associates' first job, the architects were appointed to work on a masterplan for the public spaces (unrealised) and the remodelling of the upper galleries. The artist Jennie Moncur had already installed some curvilinear floor patterns in the public spaces, and wished to develop more geometric designs for the floors of the upper galleries. Moncur asked the architects to collaborate, and in drawing up her designs they found that her intuition for squares and borders was close to a geometry that married with the formality of Nash's architecture. Together, they hit upon a square grid that aligned with the external columns and other architectural elements, and adjusted Moncur's layouts to accord with the axis of the room. Rab Bennetts describes the outcome: "We then used this grid to see if other parts of the project could be reconfigured in a similar way and we duly removed non-original additions and opened up original doors in a way that made the spaces flow…

A few years later we were appointed by the Royal College of Pathologists further down the terrace and we found that the grid could be applied equally well there. The process of removing walls and opening up internal axes on the basis of what must have been Nash's planning grid was greatly appreciated by English Heritage and the Crown Estate, who gave rapid approval."

Indeed, drawing and experiment inform every project. Pen drawings will follow a period of intense analysis of the brief, the site, the building typology; sketches and round-table brainstorming always precede computer design. An intelligent approach to computer drawing means that it isn't allowed to delude anyone about proportion or sense of space, or to imagine prematurely that the design is complete. Similarly, white foamboard models made early on, enable a loosening up of the design process, a feeling for the surfaces, volumes and light that make up a building. Such commitment to experimentation at the start of the design process, involving a number of creative minds and a strong degree of client dialogue, followed by rigorous design control throughout the construction process, has led to a highly successful body of work over the past 18 years. Whilst in recent times it has been unpropitious for architects to justify their designs in terms of aesthetics, usually preferring a functional or commercial rationale, Bennetts Associates nevertheless places quality of design at the top of the agenda. In the commercial sector of their portfolio alone, this has raised the architectural stakes greatly. Now, with the recent acclaim of their public sector cultural buildings such as the Central Library in Brighton, the practice is in a position to justify the art of architecture for its own sake as well as within the contexts

**John Menzies
Edinburgh Park**
Right: Tapestry triptych,
Susan Mowatt

Far right: Stainless steel
sculpture, Keith McCarter

BT Edinburgh Park
Opposite, left: View along
the 'street'

Opposite, middle:
Ambient Light, Adam
Barker-Mill

Opposite, right: Detail of
Beyond Words, Shona
McMullan

of cost and energy efficiency.

The Bennetts Associates' method and aesthetic is firmly shared and developed by all members of the team, a policy that should ensure its continuation. The involvement of artists – which may help fulfil or occasionally challenge this aesthetic – is one that enthuses the whole practice, and to the younger generation of architects it is acknowledged as an enriching process.

"There is no art without emotion, no emotion without passion."
Ann Bodkin of Bennetts Associates quoting Le Corbusier

"Artists can make you think about something in a completely different way." Rab Bennetts

John Menzies Edinburgh Park
One of the first buildings on site in the Edinburgh Park, masterplanned by Richard Meier with landscaping by Ian White Associates, the John Menzies headquarters appears as a sleek glass structure, reflected in the lake and in turn reflecting the surrounding landscape and skies. Perfectly proportioned, it reads almost like an abstracted Palladian facade. In some ways the building responds to the clear framework of the Meier masterplan, and, internally, there is a nod to that architect's use of minimal structural elements and love of white. Completed in 1995, its pristine state belies its age and is testimony to the client's pride in the building and high standards of maintenance, as well as the clarity of its design.

"The intention throughout was to invest the qualities of texture, light and shade within the workplace." Rab Bennetts

The atrium space, overlooked by office areas, meeting rooms and the staff restaurant, possesses a grandeur of scale mitigated by warmth in choice of materials – a pinkish French limestone floor, slatted timber seating, and wide timber balustrades.

Art was considered early on in the process, and two commissions were the outcome. The first, a tapestry by Susan Mowatt, a graduate from Edinburgh College of Art, was commissioned following research by the architects for the triple-height wall facing the staircase. This sensitive three-part work in muted colours adds softness to its surroundings; a peacock blue within its composition has been repeated by the architects on the reverse triple-height wall running through the cafe and meeting rooms. The other artwork in the building is a large scale stainless steel sculpture by Keith McCarter, which commands the northern end of the atrium, its interlocking forms acting as a foil for the rectilinear precision of the architecture. Daylight infuses the entire space, which remains admirably uncluttered. The views from the circulation route in front of the meeting rooms lead the eye through the strict elegance of Ian White's landscaping out towards the lochan, and low light in turn is reflected back off the lake into the building. From the outside at night, the perfectly proportioned rectangle of the glazed curtain wall glows with light, the effect doubled through its mirror image in the lake, an elegant elder sibling to the gutsy, colourful exterior of the BT building nearby.

BT Edinburgh Park

Declaring its presence through strong colour and form – a brilliant red cube set within a steel cylinder striated with sun screens – the BT building creates a dynamic entrance to the Edinburgh Park. It's a larger, inevitably more complex plan than Menzies, housing 900 employees rather than 200, and is organised around five atria and the cube/drum. The practice, with the client, decided on strong colours as a means of signing the building, and the brightest of several reds was chosen in preference to a more corporate blue. Prior to this Bennetts Associates had used strong colour in 1994 at the Heathrow World Business Centre where four low-budget buildings are readily identified externally at 320 kilometres per hour from the runway by their interior walls based on the colours of the spectrum: rust, jade, blue and ochre.

Artworks characterise the interior of the BT building, and whilst none of the artworks was conceived early on as part of the design or structure of the architecture, imagining the building without them immediately invokes a diminishing sense of focus and orientation. A selection panel was formed with Bennetts Associates' John Miller and the client, and each of the short-listed artists – all of them younger to mid-career artists with Scottish connections – responded to a range of sites under the broad yet appropriate theme of 'communication'.

At either end of the ground floor 'street', two artworks face each other over a distance of nearly 100 metres. A minimalist sculpture *Ambient Light* by Adam Barker-Mill incorporates three lighting slots, each subtly reacting to the shifting lighting conditions over a day. This acts as a foil to the glowing, predominantly red glass artwork *Sense* by Inge Paneels, two parallel layers of glass, the outer one incorporating a smeared red enamel circle. Two other works stand out, each monochromatic and text-based. Elizabeth Ogilvie's installation in the northern atrium comprises over 50 suspended shafts of thin glass, each set with holograms depicting a binary code. Kinetic, transparent and light-catching, this intelligent piece meets the client's and the architect's brief for an artwork that animates the space without restricting views and light, whilst inhabiting a large area and retaining its own integrity. Shona McMullan's *Beyond Words*, a large-scale wall-based textwork, is sited immediately adjacent to a staircase that both intersects the artwork and allows closer engagement with it. Its reflective metallic word-scape of figures of speech/use of language is set against a cloudscape, an allusion to the floating, indistinct nature of much communication conveyed through the spoken word.

The distinctive quality of the BT interiors is further enhanced by the installation of classic modern furniture to restaurants and public spaces.

Wessex Water Operations Centre

Sited in an area of outstanding natural beauty at the head of the valley on Claverton Down near Bath University, the first impression of Wessex Water is of a building melding with its landscape. This is a building completely at one with its setting. Transparency is key; all views are maximised, and it is possible to look right through the building into the landscape from the main entrance. The honey-coloured Bath stone of the facades softens the sharp angles of the roof structure which extend out into the landscape.

Cool tones predominate in the interior spaces, upped by the zing of vermilion seating and three coloured walls at the end of each of the office floorplates; a lime green for spring, Robin Hood green for summer, and magenta for autumn reference the landscape outside.

The landscape architects, Bernard Ede/Grant Associates, have connected the edges of the building with the landscape beyond, through wildflower and meadow planting, and green roofs. Two courtyards act as 'lungs', with their own micro-climate created through shelter and planting. These are the settings for one of the two artists commissioned for the building. Water, inevitably, was the starting point and theme for the art commissions. Of the several artists who were invited to submit proposals in response to a brief, Bettina Furnée was selected for the courtyards, and Susanna Heron for the interior 'street' and wall.

Heron's *River*, a dark, mysterious work with a commanding presence, is set within a wall facing on to the 'street', and also viewed from the steps leading down from the reception. Announcing its presence through the sound of water cascading down over striated slate, which is carved with an abstract organic form, the artwork attracts the viewer yet resists easy interpretation as a corporate 'water feature'. Rather, it is a wall-based sculpture in slate and flowing water, a 'river' as the title suggests. The dialogue between artist and architect, begun at Wessex, continued with a highly successful collaboration between Heron and Bennetts Associates at City Inn Westminster hotel.

Bettina Furnée's seating sculptures, two sets of three for each courtyard, inhabit and calibrate the terraces, acting as a counterpoint to both architecture and landscape design. Her concept involved researching quotes about water in literature and poetry, and carving selected phrases into the limestone blocks.

Loch Lomond Gateway and Orientation Centre

A single storey steel pavilion – a poetic response to the landscape, the water, and the site's industrial past – the facade of the Loch Lomond Gateway and Orientation Centre is largely screened by an untreated oak colonnade, a material now weathered silver. Setting up

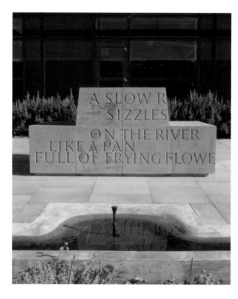

Wessex Water Operations Centre
Above left and middle: Courtyard sculptures, Bettina Furnée

Above right: Wild flowers in the new landscape

Loch Lomond Gateway and Orientation Centre
Opposite: Detail of oak colonnade

a rhythm that leads the eye towards the loch, shadows from the colonnade create strong angular patterns across the Bredon gravel. From a broad covered balcony area, there are splendid views out over the loch. This is slightly reminiscent, albeit on a smaller scale, of the framed view out over Lake Lucerne from the Concert Hall by Jean Nouvel.

As a work of architecture, Bennetts Associates' pavilion is almost reticent, ceding the star role to the loch and landscape which, after all, are its *raison d'être*, as a 'gateway' to Loch Lomond and Scotland's first National Park. Within the building, a minimal exhibition structure fulfils its purpose of conveying information on flora and fauna, and the artworks commissioned for the site.

For this scheme, a brief was drawn up and a shortlist of artists invited to propose work for the wooded promontory adjacent to the pavilion. Six artists were commissioned, and here, in keeping with the building's role as showcase for the National Park, the artists' interventions are sited within the landscape, with the exception of Olaf Nicolai, whose sustainable artwork takes the form of *matches for trees, trees for matches* within the centre's shop.

The artworks within the landscape, accessed from a wooden duckboard walkway leading from the Orientation Centre, constitute a small-scale sculpture park. Of the most notable, Vong Phaophanit's *Untitled (Field of Labels)*, colonises part of the woodland: polished steel blank 'labels' on slim masts of varying heights and angles mirror the trees, landscape and sky, offering a literal and metaphorical reflection about the nature of looking and identifying. By contrast, *Fall* by Donald Urquhart is a single, minimal Corten steel sentinel, a quiet

presence sited in the woodland close to the Orientation Centre, and obliquely referencing the architecture's calm structure and clear rectangular form. Siobhan Hapaska and Fiddian Warman's *4 Luv*, a multi-sited work on 30 trees around the loch, draws on the 'romantic' idea of carving names and initials into the bark of trees. These discreet sculptures, which at first sight could be mistaken for camouflaged bird feeders but are in fact SMS receivers, invite the viewer to text love messages.

A further, larger scale sculpture intervenes within the extraordinary loch setting: *Floodwall* by Julienne Dolphin Wilding appears at first to be a bold gesture on the 'beach' of the promontory, until it becomes evident that the sculpture marks the site of a floodwall to prevent erosion of the loch edge. The material appears unexpected – a sparkling quartz – yet is sourced locally.

The walkway leads back into the centre, where the public can access aural and visual data on the art commissions and each artist's approach to making a new, site-specific work in response to the Orientation Centre and Scotland's first National Park. The prevailing memory of the architecture and its related art programme is of modest yet affirmative mark-making within a grand landscape.

The Richard Attenborough Centre for Disability and the Arts, Leicester

In 1994 Bennetts Associates commenced two new arts buildings: the Richard Attenborough Centre for Disability and the Arts at the University of Leicester, and Hampstead Theatre in London's Swiss Cottage.

The Richard Attenborough Centre is a classic: a low cost, low energy building designed around a double-height hall, and incorporating arts facilities for all, with a special focus on people with disabilities and those with difficulties accessing the arts.

As with all Bennetts Associates' buildings, daylight is maximised in the interior and use of timber brings warmth and acoustic benefits. Built within a tight site and budget, the centre contains a wide spectrum of arts activities, and is eminently flexible in terms of interior spatial configurations for the needs of visual arts, music, dance and drama. Strong touches of colour aid orientation and guide the visually impaired. Accessibility – physical and perceptual – is paramount. This is a building that's positively welcoming – rather than merely accessible – to wheelchair users.

Externally, with its partial timber cladding, the centre appears like a Modernist music box. You almost expect it to hum or vibrate – which indeed it does much of the time, with music and dance rehearsals and performances. It connects smoothly with the University of Leicester campus, and has the air of an inevitable component within its setting, yet declares itself as a unique public arts facility. The views from the centre connect to the campus: a balcony extends nearly the full width of the main timber-clad facade. The early Stirling & Gowan Engineering Building looms nearby amongst other less distinguished neighbours. The centre's continued success, after nine years of creative activity, is testimony to the excellence and flexibility of its architectural design as well as its vibrant programme of arts activities.

Hampstead Theatre, Swiss Cottage, London

For many years, Hampstead Theatre had been housed in 'temporary' accommodation, close to Sir Basil Spence's Library and Swimming Pool. When Bennetts Associates won the competition for the theatre, they also put forward a masterplan for the site as a whole for consideration by the local authority, the London Borough of Camden. This commitment on Bennetts Associates' part to locating the new theatre within a redesigned public realm has led to the long-term arts-led regeneration for this quarter of Swiss Cottage. The local authority took up the challenge, and subsequently appointed Gustafson Porter to design the main area of landscaping/public realm, John McAslan Architects to renovate the library, and Terry Farrell Architects to design the new leisure centre. Public art being an essential component of Arts Lottery funded projects, the theatre and Bennetts Associates commissioned an art plan and, a little later, the local authority commissioned a public art strategy from the same art consultants for the whole Swiss Cottage site, thus ensuring continuity of curatorial approach.

Of the several key opportunities suggested for artists' commissions in relation to the theatre, light was agreed as a priority, and Martin Richman was subsequently appointed for the commission. His approach was to take the building as a whole and create a series of lighting interventions both inside and out; in the interior, a light wall extending along the lower ground floor area creates an appropriately dramatic setting; its colours, which are programmed to change

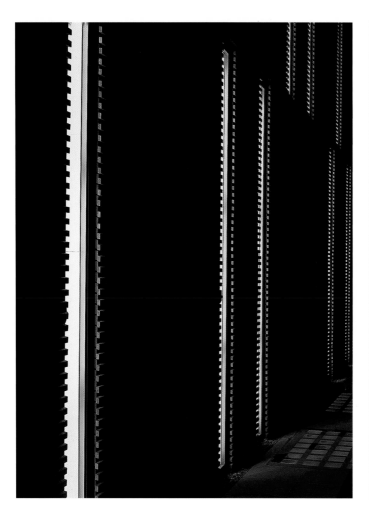

continually, reflect off the zinc surface of the auditorium drum wall. Externally, Richman has also introduced programmed coloured lighting into the glazed areas which alternate with the timber slats cladding the building. Thus the theatre is 'signed' with light. In fact, Richman's role has extended throughout the Swiss Cottage site, with further coloured lighting interventions on the redundant electricity sub-station near the Theatre, the exterior of the library and the leisure centre.

Inside the theatre two architectural elements dominate the public circulation spaces: the sculptural zinc-clad drum wall apparently bursting outwards towards the top, creates a sense of excitement and imminent action; close by, an immensely long bar adds a further sense of occasion and drama – latent danger, even, like all the best bars. By contrast, the auditorium uses softer materials, and responds to the client's brief for an intimate space, retaining the proximity of audience and actors that was a hallmark of the old theatre. Quite steeply raked, the seating combines excellent sightlines with the warm vermilion of the traditional theatre. Timber is used extensively for its acoustic and tactile values.

Externally, the theatre is also highly sculptural, with wooden louvres articulating its southern facade, and the gleaming fly-tower hovering above the main 'box' of the building. Although on the edge of the Swiss Cottage site, the theatre has been designed to connect fully with the new public spaces by Gustafson Porter, and feels very much grounded and 'meant' within its setting. When leaving the theatre at night, in that post-performance glow, you once again encounter the lightworks of Martin Richman, seamlessly part of the thrill of this new building.

Central Library, Brighton

Whereas Hampstead Theatre is strategically placed on the periphery of the site, Brighton's Central Library is located firmly at the centre of a masterplan designed by Bennetts Associates with local architects Lomax, Cassidy & Edwards. The Library forms the key element of this new piece of cityscape in the North Laine area, cleverly connecting itself to, and re-establishing, the earlier street grain. Conservationists and interest groups helped shape the brief, the location being a sensitive one, and yet agreement for an entirely contemporary library building was achieved.

The glass facade of the library offers inviting views to the grand interior space with its superb white columns and vaulting, whilst reflecting the new square with its sculptural seating, and even a glimpse of the green dome nearby. Bespoke ceramic cladding tiles of a deep, rich bluish-black colour provide a brilliant contrast to the high-tech glass curtain wall, in their handcrafted texture and varied sheen. These were inspired by the smaller glazed 'mathematical tiles' to be found on some late eighteenth and early nineteenth century vernacular houses in Brighton's Royal Crescent and elsewhere in Sussex. At roofline level, the wind towers required for this admirably low energy building add to the cityscape, making a rhythm in space.

The Library Service's brief focused on three key priorities: accessibility, flexibility and choice; the architecture achieves these priorities brilliantly, the rooms around the main space acting as an inhabited wall. Staff involvement has been key, not only in helping determine the brief, but in the final selection of materials such as the ceramic cladding, timber, furniture, colours – and art.

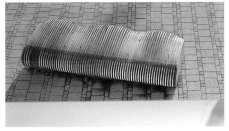

As the local authority of Brighton and Hove is client and end-user of the new Central Library, it needed to demonstrate its own public art policy, for although Brighton and Hove, like many local authorities, has a 'per cent for art' policy, it rarely applied it to its own capital projects. The procurement route was through two open competitions – one for the two Central Library art commissions, the other for the square; Bennetts Associates were involved throughout the commissioning process, having helped identify sites and commented on the briefs.

Appropriately, the two library commissions take the function of the building as the inspiration. Georgia Russell's *Uncover/Discover*, a semi-transparent artwork suspended above the entrance, takes a magnified page of dictionary definitions of 'library' as the subject.
The artist has cut into the sheet in tear/wave shaped patterns, deconstructing the surface, but allowing fragments of words/phrases /meaning to remain visible. This paper is encased within two layers of toughened glass, suspended from an elegant steel cable system. Visible from the outside and inside, the artwork casts shadows on the wall behind it, duplicating its effect.

The installation required extensive collaboration between artist, architect and engineer, and the success of this teamwork is evident; the artwork maintains its integrity yet works within its architectural setting. It enlivens the corner of the building, being visible across the square and from Jubilee Street. At night, a vertical light beam scans across the artwork slowly from left to right, animating the facade of the library.

A contemporary cathedral to knowledge, ideas and information, the central area of the library breathes light, its eight columns the sole support of the first floor floating above, whose columns in turn support the roof structure. The white vaulting above, like fans or propellers, suggest gravity-defying weightlessness. Everywhere, tactile materials and data enable the visually impaired – the most disadvantaged group for the library sector – to orientate and locate data. The door signage symbols are all tactile (Gill Sans), Braille is used only on the washroom doors.

Beech walls add warmth and acoustic qualities; deep green carpets sooth the eye whilst brighter hues are to be found in the washrooms. But the deepest, most magical colour is the intense blue of the children's library back wall, selected by the ceramicist, Kate Malone, as the backdrop for her *Wall of a Thousand Stories*. The brief called for the artwork to be an inspiration for story-telling and Malone's firmament of ceramic reliefs depicts visual elements drawn from thirty different categories, including nature, animals, music, magic, theatre, landscape. These imaginative ceramics are designed to be touched.

Events such as 'A Big Read' and other activities generated by the library extend to its new domain of Jubilee Square, reinforcing the masterplan's intention to connect the building to its external environment, especially during the Brighton Festival. This is reinforced by the limestone linking interior to exterior, and to a larger extent by the third art commission by Caroline Barton. In her winning submission, the artist chose to 'place' objects within the square rather than to intervene fundamentally with its materials. Entitled *Liquidus*, the sculptural seats are formed from layers of sweet chestnut and a clear acrylic; lit from within, these amoeba-like forms glow at night, animating the public space.

The Brighton Central Library exudes style and glamour of a

Central Library, Brighton
Left: *Wall of a Thousand Stories*, Kate Malone

City Inn Westminster
Right: Views of *Side Street*, Susannah Heron

long-lasting kind. This is another Bennetts Associates 'classic', which should influence this building type in the future.

City Inn Westminster

The multiple award-winning City Inn hotel, close to Tate Britain, represents two 'firsts' for Bennetts Associates – as well as being their first hotel, the project delivered the first opportunity for them to consider the artist's role as a fundamental element in the design of a new public space. Occupying a long-empty site, the building's plan makes sense of a strangely shaped 'footprint', which successfully reconnects the Embankment to the surrounding area whilst respecting the local street grain. Like all successful buildings, it has an air both of surprise and inevitability.

The visual hallmarks of Bennetts Associates' architecture are seen in the restrained elegance of the hotel's main facade on John Islip Street with its glazed wall and sun-screens. Set back from the pavement, the scale and density required of this building type are offset by the sensitivity of the architecture to its surrounding environment. A new piece of cityscape has effectively been created, combining the geometric rigour of the architecture with permeability and legibility.

A cobalt blue flank wall on the external architectural envelope, reminiscent of the blue used by Scarpa in the Fondazione Masieri in Venice, contrasts with the warmth of strong reds in many interior spaces (furniture in the main bar and soffit level lighting in the reception area), and the timber floors and doors. There is a generosity of proportion to the publicly accessible areas of the hotel at ground and

first floor levels, and the Sky Bar has become known as one of London's best new party venues, with its panoramic views out over the Thames.

Access to the hotel's foyers, restaurant and bars is enhanced by the public's usage of the new pedestrian 'cut' from John Islip Street to Thorney Street and the Embankment. This space is the site of a large-scale environmental artwork by Susanna Heron.

Careful tactics are required by architects in order to introduce the notion of an art strategy; too early and the client may not 'buy into it'; too late, and the scope for collaboration and integration is minimised, and the art becomes an afterthought. But at City Inn, two major factors (in addition to the architects' commitment) contributed to the successful early involvement of an artist. The client, the Orr family, has a long track record of supporting the arts, and they embraced whole-heartedly the chance to engage an artist as part of the design team. Second, Westminster City Council's public art policy strongly encourages inward investors to commission public art. Soon an art strategy was commissioned, and of several sites proposed, the new pedestrian route was chosen as offering greatest artistic scope.

The design of this covered 'street' became the subject for a brief to artists drawn up by the art consultants with input from the architects and the client. Following competitive interviews, Susanna Heron was appointed to develop designs, in close collaboration with the architects. The final artwork is a new place: a long glazed pedestrian route, every element of which has been subject to the artist's creative scrutiny. She observed that "the area has a strong history of social reform and still hosts major institutions for central government, art, religion and education alongside extensive areas

of housing… the general public who visit the street will be extraordinarily varied… The street, then, would act as both route and destination." Her aim was "to make the whole street a living work of art in association with the architects".

Heron and David Olson of Bennetts Associates together considered the design and materials of the glazed roof, the pavement materials, the changing effects of daylight and artificial lighting on the entire space – not least upon Heron's carved slate wall reliefs on the western wall, beneath which are located minimal seating slabs. Heron introduced a series of non load-bearing white columns as further sculptural/spatial elements to articulate the route and to demarcate the outside cafe space with its elegant Arad *Tom Vac* chairs, from the main pedestrian area. Two magnolia grandiflora trees further pinpoint the journey, at the change in angle of *Side Street* – the title for this work of environmental sculpture.

Heron's relief sculptures in slate extend her fascination with organic forms, previously seen at the British Embassy in Dublin, Hackney Community College in London, in Tokyo and as part of the Phoenix Initiative in Coventry. These are 'slow burn' artworks, according to Heron; she likes "the fact that you can make a subtle work in the public domain that accumulates over a period of years. It must survive the utilitarian nature of the environment… I like the idea that people come across my work by chance."

Indeed, many people do discover this magical place 'by chance' yet return here again and again. *Side Street* sets up a series of rhythms and contrasts: transparency and opacity, light and shadow, organic and orthogonal forms.

Artworks selected by the client, David Orr, decorate the restaurant and other public areas. Indeed, City Inn has become known as an 'arts hotel', with the Tate Gallery and Frieze Art Fair among its regular clientele. Heron's *Side Street* has been a major catalyst in this successful marketing strategy.

New Street Square, City of London

From 2003, Bennetts Associates has increasingly introduced the possibility of art commissions early on in the masterplanning process, with the aim of integrating artists' work in public space as well as in relation to architecture. Masterplans for City Road Basin in Islington, London, 2003, and Potterrow, Edinburgh, 2003, facilitate this commitment to collaborations with artists. Bennetts Associates' designs for the London 2012 Olympic Aquatics Centre, 2004, contained an Art Strategy as an essential component of the submission. In 2002, the Devonshire Square development commissioned by AXA Insurance triggered a competition for an artist's design of the adjacent public space; won by Paul de Monchaux with a sculptural treatment of the whole space, this proposal was sadly never implemented.

One of the most ambitious public art/public space/architecture schemes to date in the practice's portfolio is the New Street Square project for Land Securities Plc. Strictly defined as private land but with comprehensive public access at street level, the New Street Square development comprises five new buildings including a small 'pavilion', and public routes to and through the new square. Located in the legal quarter of the City, New Street Square falls within the Corporation of London's domain and its Fleet Street Courts and Lanes Strategy.

The architects' intention has been to design a scheme that "respected and engaged with the urban context rather than being purely inward-looking". One of the key aims, as well as providing high quality office accommodation and restaurant and retail at ground level, was to "create a new and vibrant public space within the development… providing a distinct identity for the area and supporting the existing urban pattern". Bennetts' design strategy was based on buildings of varying heights around a piazza. Cleverly addressing the need to reinstate desire lines across the development, the four routes into and from the square are appropriately of human, intimate scale; you discover the new public place, rather than having the route dictated. In plan, a pinwheel effect is created, with the routes radiating out from the square, with the buildings as backdrop to this new urban stage. This arrangement is comparable to the oblique routes into Campo Santa Margharita in Venice, which you happen upon almost by chance. Cited by Camillo Sitte in his *City Planning according to Artistic Principles*, Campo Santa Margharita is one of Venice's – and possibly Europe's – most successful public spaces, due to its asymmetry and informality.

A study commissioned by Bennetts Associates from the London School of Economics' Cities Programme on public usage of this area informed the practice's thinking about the site; further research into successful public places was undertaken by the architects in their "Genius Loci" document. In 2004, the client commissioned a Public Art Strategy, which researched international precedents for public-art-as-public-space, also historical and contemporary material about the area that artists might draw upon in their proposals.

A generic brief was produced as part of the public art strategy, outlining the scope of opportunities for artists, including the design of the square, a commemorative commission to Dr Johnson (the Johnson Museum being located nearby) and the potential for an artist/architect collaboration on the design of the pavilion.

Of the five artists invited to produce detailed designs, two – Vito Acconci and Tobias Rehberger – were retained for intensive design workshops with the architects. The final selection of Vito Acconci to progress a collaborative design with Bennetts Associates reflects the desire on the part of the client and design team for an artist's full engagement with the square as a public space and its potential connection with the wider public realm.

The notion of public art conceived as public space, rather than simply art placed within 'the public realm', is now well established internationally, although few examples exist in Britain as yet. Inevitably, the terms 'public art' and 'public realm' call into question the definition of 'public' as well as the relationship between art, space and architecture. According to Donald Judd, "Space is made by an artist or architect; it is not found and packaged. It is made by thought." [1]

The success of New Street Square will rely not just upon the quality of its architecture and art, but how it will be enlivened by those who work and live in the locality, and then how it will enter the wider public's mental map of London. Bennetts Associates' awareness of the wider environmental and sociological issues is demonstrated in the thorough research preceding all their architectural and masterplanning schemes. Whether large scale, like New Street Square, City Road Basin, Potterrow and the Royal Shakespeare Theatre or small scale, as in the design of the architects' own offices in Clerkenwell, there is a clear commitment to the place making that defines our cities. The role of artists has become an increasingly vital strand in this creative process.

Notes
1 Judd, Donald, "Some Aspects of Color in General and Red and Black in Particular", *Artforum,* Summer 1994.

City Inn Westminster
Left: View of *Side Street*,
Susanna Heron

**New Street Square,
City of London**
Above: Design studies
by Vito Acconci

PROJECTS P–Z

Peel Park

Top: Perspective of a typical office pavilion, showing the close relationship of landscape to building

Above: Sectional perspective

Left: View from the point of entry to the landscape from the car park area

Right: Site layout. Existing elements include the car park, loop road and buildings shown shaded

PEEL PARK
BLACKPOOL, 2003

This competition-winning scheme redefines an existing high-security business park on the outskirts of Blackpool through the addition of several new office pavilions around a central landscape.

The site has a sense of incompleteness, with only part of the business park's first phase having been completed. Despite the small number of buildings, there is extensive car park provision that can cope with all future expansion, so Bennetts Associates' scheme is entirely devoted to new buildings and landscape rather than to any further parking.

The design creates a coherent sense of place, by arranging the additional offices around the perimeter of the site as the enclosure to a completely new landscape in the centre of the park. The buildings themselves are straightforward and classically simple, to allow the communal open space to dominate. The landscape includes water bodies to deal with natural drainage and water retention, combined with indigenous planting and a range of informal trails. A more formal boardwalk at the outer margin of the open space links the entrances and open courtyards of the new development.

The new buildings themselves are designed for minimum environmental impact, with low operational and embodied carbon dioxide emissions. Using research pioneered on the Wessex Water and New Street Square projects, the form of construction exploits 'passive' engineering solutions as far as possible, but retains the possibility of 'active' systems with floor-based ventilation where required. The courtyard at the centre of each building facilitates natural ventilation and extends the impact of the landscape into the setting of the workplace. Overall flexibility in the services options and in the floorplate layouts is seen as essential to long-term sustainability.

PowerGen Headquarters

Above: Construction view showing the profile and quality of the in situ concrete coffers

Right: Tapered steel reinforcement cages

Opposite: North-south section

POWERGEN HEADQUARTERS
COVENTRY, 1991–94

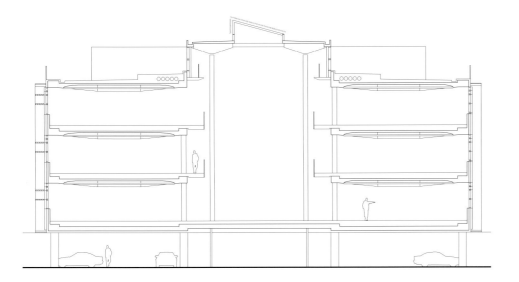

The PowerGen Headquarters has been described as the most influential office building of the 1990s.

Among the many dramatic changes affecting the electricity industry following privatisation, PowerGen required a far more efficient working environment for their core staff, commensurate with their need to focus on operational costs and re-integration of a previously dispersed organisation. This led to a design which considers the workplace to be pre-eminent and, in challenging the conventional wisdom of 1980s office space, incorporates narrow depth of office space, clearly defined circulation routes, energy efficiency, local control over the environment and visual stimulus.

Extensive analysis of working patterns, daylight and ventilation led to a prototypical floorplate around 12 metres in width and 43 metres in length, with a circulation route placed along one side to avoid fragmenting the predominantly open plan area. Natural ventilation and an exposed, vaulted concrete structure allow a clear span across the office space and provide sufficient thermal mass for 'passive' cooling on hot summer days.

The main body of the building comprises 12 identical floorplates arranged on three floors around a linear atrium in response to a detailed Space Syntax analysis. Timber-clad towers – containing stairs, small kitchens and business centres – provide busy focal points at all levels that support the principle of unsolicited contact between different people within the organisation. With the principal floorplates grouped in the centre, the building terminates with the main entrance, conference rooms and restaurant at one end and facilities reception, computer suite and energy management centre for the company's power stations at the other.

The building is orientated east-west for optimum solar control on the main facades, with uninterrupted landscape to the north and parking to the south.

Quite apart from its impact on the office sector, the project has had a major influence on Bennetts Associates. It was the first in a continuous stream of corporate headquarters which, in contrast to buildings for development companies, allowed the firm to study in depth the requirements of actual users and building performance. It was also the project that validated much of Bennetts Associates' work on energy efficiency by way of rigorous analysis, leading the firm into extensive further research on subsequent projects. At PowerGen's insistence, it was the practice's first experience of a large design-build contract – one which proved enjoyable and highly effective, leading the firm to propose the same contracting method on many future projects.

**PowerGen
Headquarters**
Above: General view
of atrium space

Right: Reflected plan
and section of structural
bay. The in situ concrete
coffers integrate structural
requirements with those
of acoustics, lighting
and economy

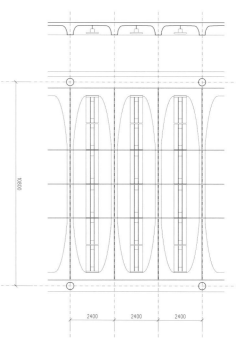

PowerGen Headquarters

Above, left: An informal meeting space

Above, centre and right: Details of the atrium stair towers

Left: The atrium at ground level

PowerGen
Headquarters
Left: South elevation

Below: Typical plan

Opposite: Detail at the
junction of the main
elevation with one of the
external fire escape stairs

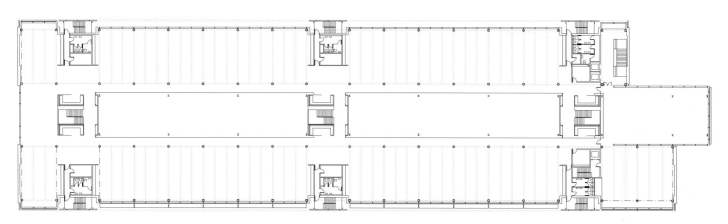

**Rail Traffic
Control Centres**
Above: The West Coast
Main Line facility at
Saltley, Birmingham

Right: The control room
at Saltley

Opposite, left: Upper
floor plan of the Saltley
building

Opposite, right top:
Montage of the London
control centre

Opposite, right below:
Saltley interior

RAIL TRAFFIC CONTROL CENTRES
BIRMINGHAM AND LONDON, 2000 –

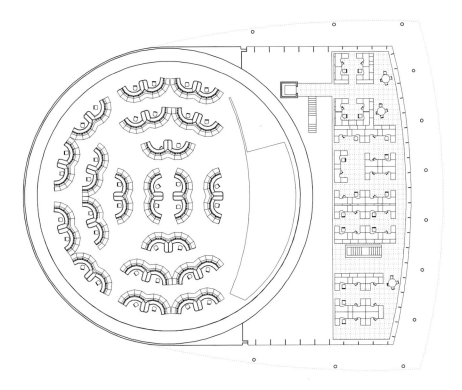

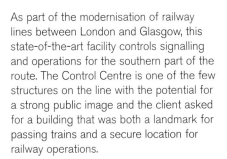

As part of the modernisation of railway lines between London and Glasgow, this state-of-the-art facility controls signalling and operations for the southern part of the route. The Control Centre is one of the few structures on the line with the potential for a strong public image and the client asked for a building that was both a landmark for passing trains and a secure location for railway operations.

The building is raised up to the level of the adjacent tracks on a plinth containing plant which is partially buried into the site. The operations room sits directly above and is encased in a secure concrete drum, topped with a domed concrete ceiling. When the new West Coast Main Line is operational, the drum will accommodate groups of signal operators equipped with computers and network display facilities in an innovative 'organic' layout.

In contrast to the solid volume and explicit security of the drum, support and management facilities are provided in a transparent two-storey glazed space that sits between the operations room and the adjacent railway line.

This was the first railway infrastructure building completed by Bennetts Associates and it has since led to a wide range of further work on the Thameslink and Crossrail projects in London.

Also illustrated here is the City Control Centre for Thameslink, London, 2003-, proposed for the railway viaduct near Tate Modern. Although similar in some respects to the West Coast Rail Traffic Control Centre, it is in essence an elevated box, clad in Corten steel.

READING OFFICE DEVELOPMENT
BERKSHIRE, 1987–89

Within a few weeks of commencing in practice in 1987, Bennetts Associates was commissioned to design this 10,000 square metre office development on the outskirts of Reading. The scale and speed of the project enabled the firm to develop its ideas for the design process, with a systematic analysis preceding design itself. Objective examination of alternative office floorplates, servicing systems and site layouts involved the whole design team and the client, leading to a rational building form that was both architecturally and commercially robust.

The building comprises two parallel wings of deep-plan office space over three floors, with an atrium, lifts and the main service-core in between. Although primarily intended for a single occupier, each floor can be sub-divided into four separate tenancies, with air-conditioning distributed from four freestanding plantroom pods at roof level.

To avoid the impression of being surrounded by a sea of cars, the building is raised up by one storey with parking below and a wide strip of land around the perimeter devoted to landscaped embankments, one of which acts as a tree-lined approach to the main entrance. The remainder of the car park is screened by a regular grid of trees and extensive hedging.

The form of the building is closely tied to its spatial arrangement and its method of construction. Difficulties with steel supplies in the late 1980s presented an opportunity for Bennetts Associates to explore what were then innovative structural solutions; the development of a precast concrete frame allows the asymmetrical layout of beams to be integrated with the pattern of services distribution and internal circulation. At roof level, long spans are reflected in barrel-vaulted profiles, with the plantrooms located on the short spans above the main distribution ducts. The synthesis of space, structure and services provides the basis for its architectural language, thereby avoiding the 'facadism' that often characterises commercial developments of this kind.

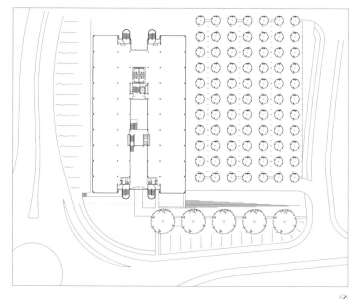

Reading Office Development
Above, left: Entrance elevation. The spatial order of the building is reflected in its external form

Above, right: Site layout. Car parking extends below the building and is screened by landscaped embankments and a grid of trees

Opposite: The ramped approach to the main entrance with imported mature trees

Reading Office Development
Above: The glazed entrance facade

Above, right (top): View of model

Above, right (below): The construction process is expressed in the form of the building

Below: Cross section. Structure, services and internal space are closely integrated

Opposite: The atrium and its circulation tower

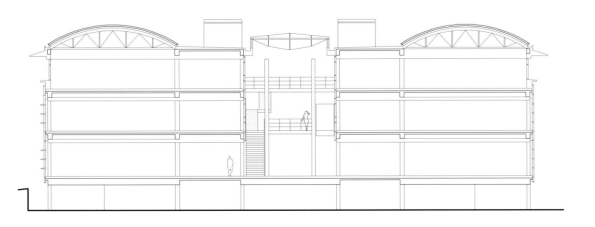

The Richard Attenborough Centre for Disability and the Arts
Above: Visual arts studio

Right: The junction between the three parts of the building

Far right: The double-height hall

THE RICHARD ATTENBOROUGH CENTRE
FOR DISABILITY AND THE ARTS
UNIVERSITY OF LEICESTER, 1994–97

The Richard Attenborough Centre is an arts building open to all, with its focus on people with disabilities and members of the public who have previously found access to arts education difficult. The centre offers courses in art, sculpture, music, dance and drama and higher degree work to encourage participation and performance to a professional standard.

The building was the result of an open competition won by Ian Taylor, a longstanding architect with Bennetts Associates, and the final building was executed by Bennetts Associates with Ian as project architect.

The building is split into three differently constructed parts. The top-lit walled structure for the rear block is separated from the steel framed front block by a double-height hall, topped by an all glass structural rooflight. The interior is designed to aid the orientation and comfort of users by manipulation of natural light, volumes and acoustics, underpinned by consistent changes within a limited range of materials. The resultant visual and acoustic character of the spaces reflects their contrasting use; recitals, dance, painting and sculpture, library, foyer and offices. It is a totally accessible environment that avoids aesthetic compromise.

Externally, the different volumes are expressed by the use of brick or timber cladding, with the structural rooflight highlighting the contrast between front and rear activities. The height of this element was calculated to screen an adjacent laboratory building when viewed from the street and to catch sunlight for the interior.

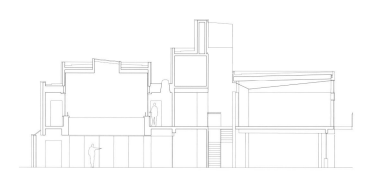

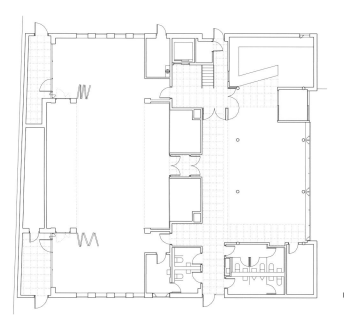

The Richard Attenborough Centre for Disability and the Arts
Above: The building in context

Left, above: Section

Left, below: Ground floor plan

THE ROYAL COLLEGE OF PATHOLOGISTS LONDON, 1991–93 AND 2004–

This project entailed extensive internal remodelling of a Grade I listed building to provide a sequence of public and private spaces for a professional institution.

The scale of Carlton House Terrace overlooking the Mall reflects its status as the last major element of Nash's grand plan for London, but Number 2 Carlton House Terrace had suffered from wartime bombing followed by an unsympathetic reconstruction. The refurbishment of the Royal College of Pathologists restores the Regency interior to its original proportions, using a modern approach to materials and details.

Clarification of internal spaces is achieved in two ways; first, by arranging the college's public and private functions on different floors to reflect the building's underlying hierarchy and, second, by recreating a clear sequence of major and minor spaces on each floor in accordance with Nash's planning grid.

At the centre of the property, a lightwell is reconstructed to create additional top-lit space on the ground floor and to restore the feeling of a piano nobile at first floor level.

As there were no remaining Regency features internally, the Crown Estate and English Heritage supported proposals for a modern aesthetic that incorporates the requirements of a fully equipped conference suite with air-conditioning. A simple palette of maple joinery, painted surfaces and an aluminium picture rail/cornice enable the splendid proportions and light within each room to speak for themselves. New wall linings stop short of internal corners to express the form of construction and to provide a modern equivalent of pilasters for visual definition.

In 2004, Bennetts Associates began work on remodelling the previously untouched basement, with the addition of a meetings and function suite within its tall brick vaults and passageways.

The Royal College of Pathologists
Right: Cross section, with the Mall on the left and Carlton House Terrace on the right. The new staircase and basement works form the second phase begun in 2004

Opposite: Detail view of one of the lecture spaces

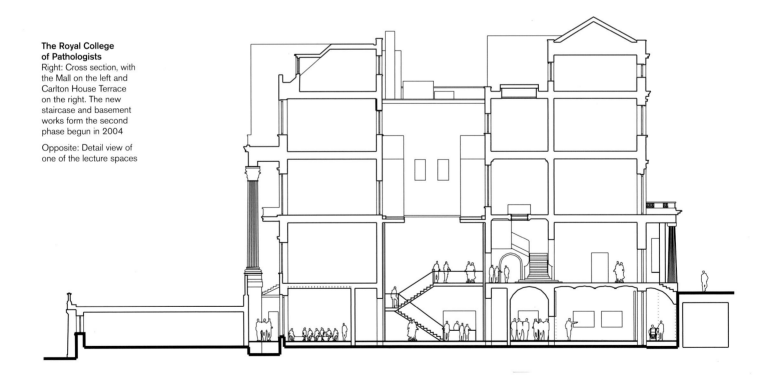

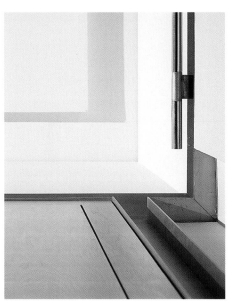

**The Royal College
of Pathologists**
Above: View of the
terrace from the Mall and
general interior views
showing maple joinery
and glass reinforced
cement lighting baffles in
the main lecture room

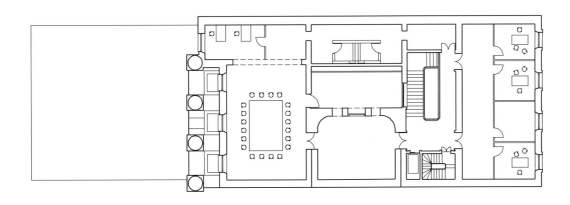

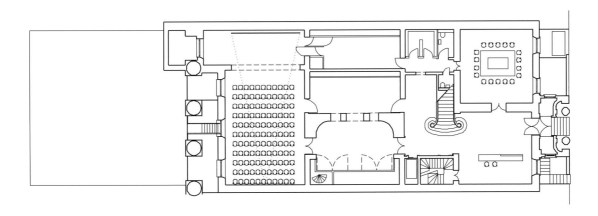

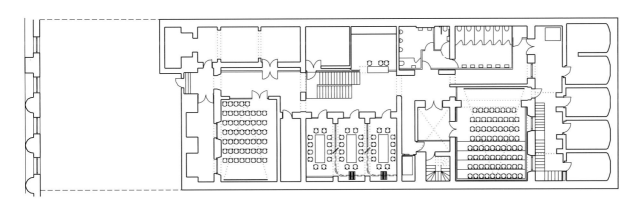

**The Royal College
of Pathologists**
From above: First floor
plan; ground floor plan;
basement plan

SOPHOS HEADQUARTERS
ABINGDON, 2000–03

Sophos Headquarters
Right: Office atrium on
first floor. The two atria
are used as training areas

Below: Section

Opposite:
The entrance hall

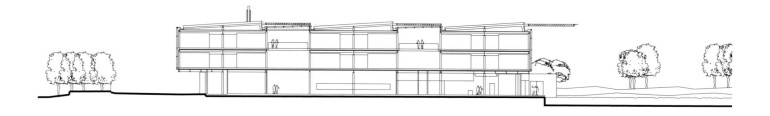

A visual language of cantilevers and curves is used to dramatise the headquarters of this fast-growing IT company.

Sophos, who specialise in anti-virus software, required a new building that would provide for expansion and enhance staff recruitment in a competitive industry, so the brief for the project emphasised external image as much as the nature of the accommodation. To achieve this, the design manipulates the external form of the building and the layout of the site to create immediate impact on arrival, without compromising the internal functions of the building.

Located in a business estate with no architectural coherence, the project establishes a dominant presence at the far end of its site, with a strong pattern of new landscape establishing the foreground on the direction of approach.

The accommodation itself comprises two relatively conventional office floors above

a deep-plan ground floor devoted to non-office functions such as conference spaces, the main restaurant, packaging areas for the company's mail order business, storage and plant. The form of the building accentuates the difference between these typologies and, whilst the steel-framed offices take the form of simple rectangles, the ground floor has an irregular, sinuous perimeter. At times, the rectangles cantilever over the curves or draw back to form a landscaped roof, the projecting structure avoiding any obvious means of support to heighten the illusion.

The ground floor perimeter is defined on its northern and eastern sides by a full-height, raking brick wall and, on the southern and western sides, by a lake. Together these two items provide physical security and the curves required of vehicle circulation; entry can only be gained across a bridge that continues the axis of the main pedestrian approach beside the car park. Conference suites and the restaurant occupy the prime locations beside the water.

The office floors are fully glazed, to capitalise on good views of the Thames and the Oxfordshire countryside in the middle distance. Because of the large numbers of computers and the need for 24-hour working, the building is air-conditioned and has less need for the thermal mass that is characteristic of previous Bennetts Associates' office projects. Nevertheless, heat gains are reduced by virtue of external solar shading, which extends up to nine metres beyond the building to ensure that the glass is fully shaded at the height of summer. Internally, the office floors are arranged to avoid large expanses of unbroken office space, with two atrium spaces acting as training and break out spaces. On the western edge of the office space, a pair of glass meeting rooms project into the three-storey high entrance space.

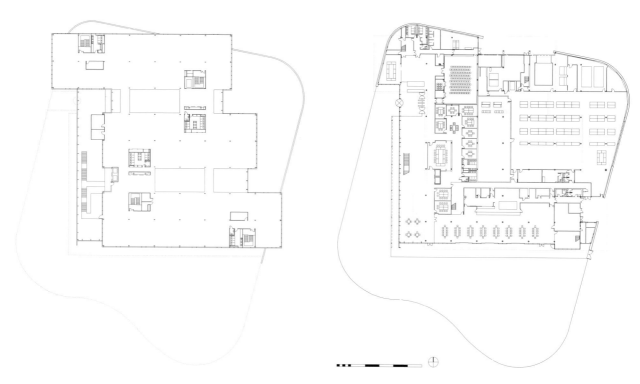

Sophos Headquarters
Above, top: Details of the raking brick wall that wraps around the building

Left: External solar shading extends up to nine metres beyond the building envelope

Opposite, above: Approach to the building at dusk

Opposite, below (left to right): Second floor plan; ground floor plan

University Departments, Potterrow

Above: The building viewed from Bristo Place, with the Appleton Tower in the distance. The landscaped area in the foreground is due to be reconfigured as part of an overall masterplan

Right: Montage from George Square

Opposite: Location plan

UNIVERSITY DEPARTMENTS, POTTERROW
EDINBURGH, 2003–

40 years after the curtailment of the Basil Spence scheme for Edinburgh University's city centre campus, a substantial new building is planned for the largest site that was cleared for development in the 1960s. As the major component of the University's new masterplan for the George Square/Bristo Square area, it replaces a windswept car park with a rich mix of buildings, courtyards and reinstated streetlines.

The new development totals approximately 25,000 square metres and there are three principal users – the School of Informatics, the College of Humanities and Social Science and University Student Support Services. In broad terms, Informatics occupies one building with the remaining users in another, but the scheme also includes street level shops, a cafe and a gallery. Each of these two primary volumes is planned round

an atrium, facing each other across a shared courtyard, but their form allows them to overlap on the street edges and undulate in height from three floors to eight. From the inside, the buildings are rational and simple; from the outside they appear far more complex and responsive to their surroundings.

A public pedestrian route passes through the courtyard on its way from Bristo Square to Potterrow, echoing the historic alignment of Bristo Street.

The academic space is relatively uniform and, unlike much of the University's estate, readily adaptable to potential future uses. Much of the accommodation is cellular, so the floorplates have been laid out to ensure that circulation routes engage with a variety of viewing points, open-plan break out spaces and double-height volumes.

Construction reflects the simplicity of the plan, with a low energy strategy based on exposed concrete slabs and air supplied from the floor supplemented by opening windows.

Externally, the elevations play on the distinction between the stone-faced streets of Edinburgh and the need for more light-reflective surfaces to the courtyard. Different types of stone cladding and contrasting ratios of solid to void are used to highlight the hierarchy implied by the different facades, Charles Street being the major thoroughfare with the greatest need for animation and Potterrow being more regular. A similar pattern of storey-height panels is used in the courtyard spaces, but with quartz-aggregate white concrete providing a tone and atmosphere more suited to external spaces in a northern climate.

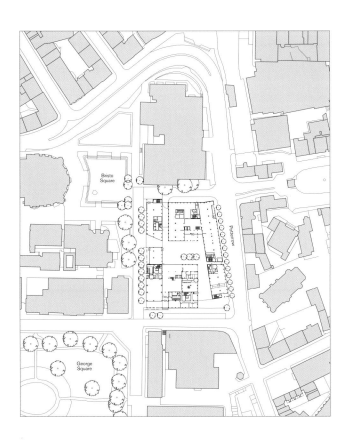

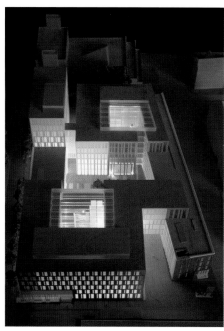

University Departments, Potterrow
Left and far left: Final model

Below: Fourth floor plan. Informatics occupies the southern atrium building, with Social Science and Student Support Services occupying the remainder

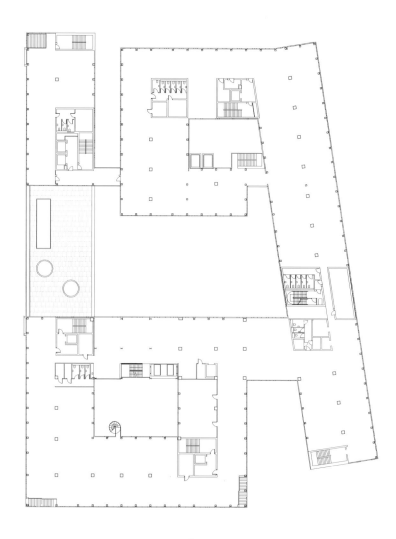

University Departments, Potterrow

Above: Views of an early massing model

Below: East elevation to Potterrow

Below: West elevation to Charles Street. George Square is to the right

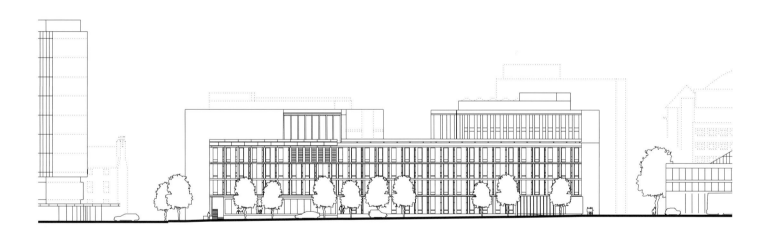

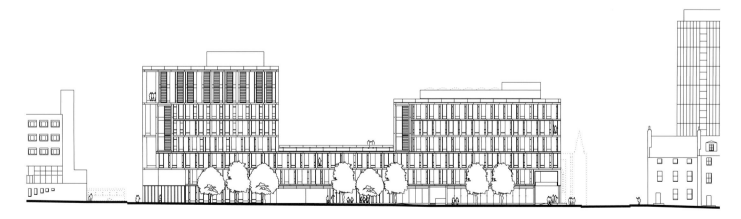

WATERLOO BUS STATION
LONDON, 2003

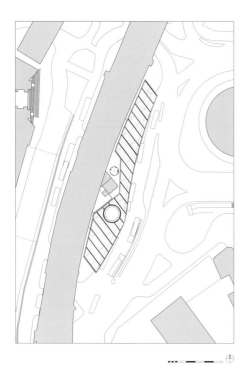

This key transport interchange lies adjacent to the rail terminus and serves thousands of commuters daily. Under these proposals the facility is given a fresh identity to match its status through provision of a canopy and enhanced passenger facilities.

The new structure extends over the entire pedestrian area and the irregular shape of the roof reflects the curving alignment of bus roadways on one side and a series of existing obstructions on the other. The largest of these is the railway viaduct, but the canopy also circumvents a large vent shaft from the Jubilee Underground line and a listed public house that is the relic of a pre-railway terrace.

The choice of translucent ETFE pillows for the canopy roof allows views and high levels of daylight for passengers emerging from the railway viaduct arches without high cost or maintenance. The repetitive structural grid provides a degree of standardisation for a relatively complex shape and enables columns to fit comfortably within pedestrian circulation routes. To keep the canopy free of visual clutter, the Y-shaped columns contain only rainwater drainage, with lighting and signage confined to ground level screens or seating assemblies. Planning permission was obtained in 2003.

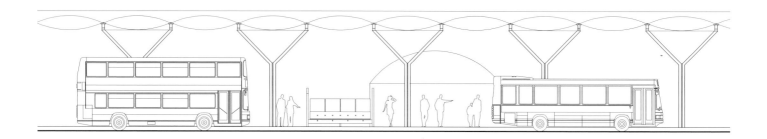

Waterloo Bus Station
Above: Montage showing
how the canopy avoids
existing obstructions

Right: View from the
rail station exit through
the canopy

Opposite, above:
Site plan

Opposite, below:
Part elevation

WESSEX WATER OPERATIONS CENTRE
BATH, 1998–2001

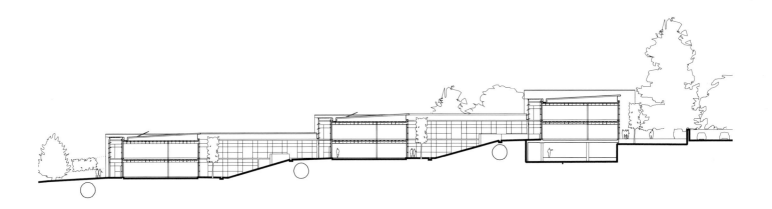

This project was the fourth in a series of major headquarters by Bennetts Associates that were intended to show, first, how architectural form had a critical role to play in the design of the workplace and, second, how sustainability was consistent with design at the highest level.

The project was acclaimed by the Building Research Establishment as the 'greenest' commercial building in the United Kingdom, and its sustainability credentials are well documented through publications and research papers. The building has been the subject of extensive post-occupancy assessment, which has validated the original strategy behind its environmental design.

However, the form of the building and its landscape also show a clear evolution from the direct architectural language of

PowerGen in the early 1990s to a more complex idiom of spaces, courts, views and construction techniques that reflects the UK's greater level of economic self-assurance at the end of the decade.

Located on a steeply sloping site in a designated Area of Outstanding Natural Beauty, the building adopts a low profile, barely protruding above the existing stone walls that once surrounded a small isolation hospital. Most of the office accommodation is absorbed in three uniform wings that adopt an E shape on plan, each wing facing the sun and looking over the roof of the one below. Running down the slope in parallel is a range of communal spaces – an operations room, meeting rooms, a boardroom and catering facilities – that provide a visual foil to the office space and a malleable form that can follow the boundary wall. In between the

offices and the communal areas is a top-lit, linear space that gets progressively narrower as it descends the contours from the main entrance to the woodland at the foot of the site. Glimpses into the offices are complemented by framed views between the communal rooms to the fields beyond. This forum-like space is the mechanism for binding the disparate parts of the building together and is the location for impromptu meetings, social gatherings and special events.

Construction of the building breaks new ground in terms of embodied energy and off-site prefabrication, resulting in a visual lightness that is a metaphor for the building's impact on its surroundings. The use of local Bath stone and the careful preservation of existing trees reinforces the impression of a building that is at ease in its surroundings.

**Wessex Water
Operations Centre**
Opposite: North-south
section. Rainwater
retention tanks are shown
below each courtyard

Above: Looking north
from the space outside
the restaurant

Right: View in the
direction of Salisbury
Plain. The site was
previously an isolation
hospital

Wessex Water Operations Centre

Above: The street viewed from upper level

Far left: Office space, viewed from the street. The steel beams are perforated to enhance airflow at high level

Left: The board room, glimpsed from the street

Opposite (from below right, clockwise): Level 1 plan, level 2 plan, level 3 plan, level 4 plan

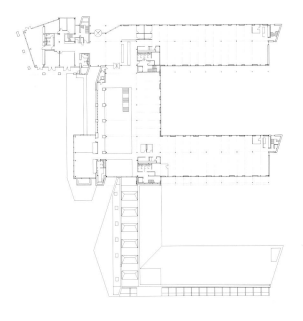

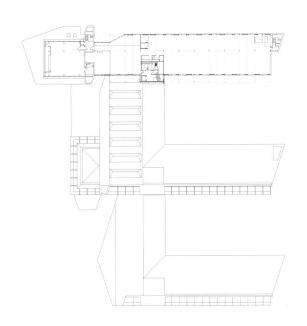

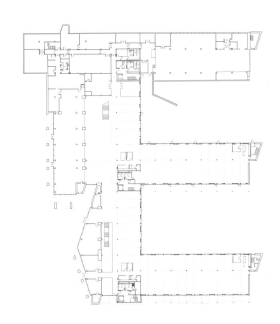

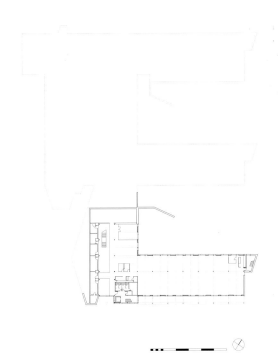

**Wessex Water
Operations Centre**
Left: The central street
looking north towards
the main entrance

Below: Lightweight
concrete coffers being
hoisted in to place

Below, left: The recently
completed structure

Below, right: Reflected
plan and section of
structural bay, showing
light steel framework,
precast concrete units
and lighting rafts

Opposite: Aluminium
solar shading to the
south elevation

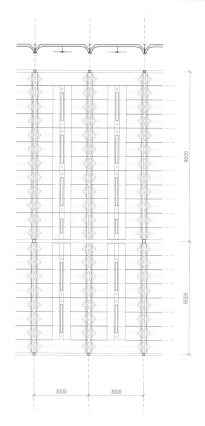

PETER CAROLIN
SYNTHESIS AND TRADITION

The concluding essay in this book takes a broad overview of Bennetts Associates' approach and its most prominent buildings over the last decade. As the title suggests, Peter Carolin brings together the traditional architectural virtues with those of current practice, showing why qualities such as place making, gravitas or enjoyment and the need for competent delivery or fitness for purpose are not mutually exclusive. He also describes from his own experience the impact of the buildings on visitors and on the all-important users, so often neglected by architectural critics and image-makers alike. To illustrate his essay, Carolin draws out themes that unite the firm's work, including sustainability and what he describes as the art of construction, noting that many buildings, both in the public and private sectors, have been procured at speed in a fierce commercial milieu. He concludes by observing that quality of architecture and technique are inseparable for this practice and that the results are invariably humane, respectful and significant.

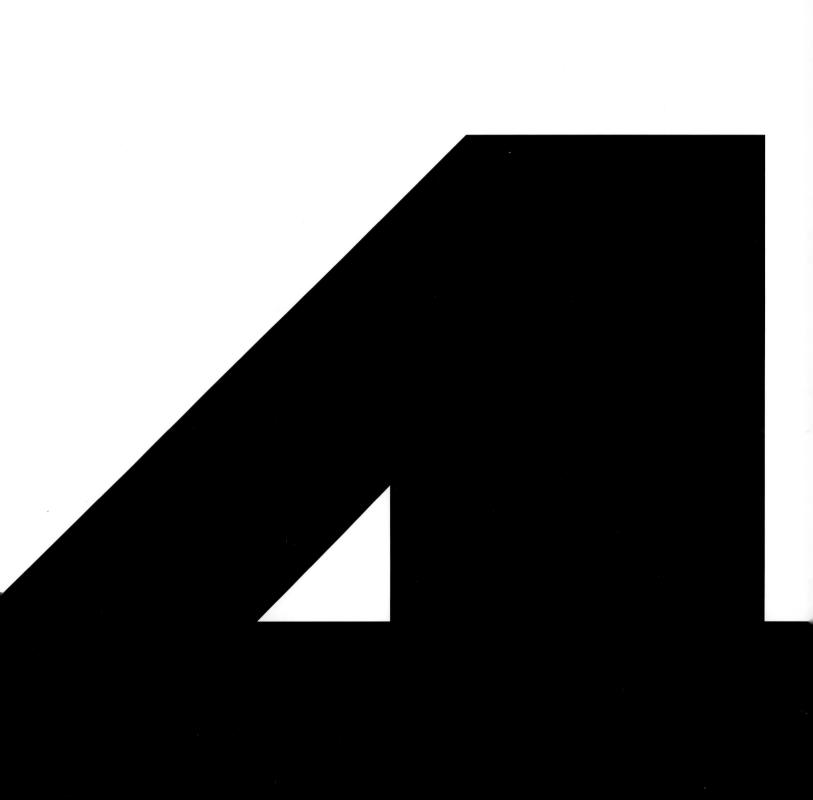

4

The publication of PowerGen in 1995 propelled Bennetts Associates into the limelight. Conceived by a small, 12-strong practice for one of the giants of privatised industry, the new building raised the design of offices to an entirely new level. In the decade since, the practice has completed several other significant offices and has, understandably, become more closely associated with this building type than any other.

A powerful strand of evolutionary development relates these offices to each other. This can be seen in the arrangement of the parts that combine to form the anatomy of each particular building. It is also apparent in elements such as the ceiling-plane of those that are not air-conditioned. But, despite the evolutionary lineage, there is an astonishing variety about these designs. Each of them reads as a specific solution exploiting to the full what Rab Bennetts has described as "the traditional raw materials of architecture – shape, colour, daylight, circulation routes, meeting places and so on".

But to associate this group of architects with offices alone is to do it a disservice for it has also successfully completed both an impressive range of other building types and many masterplans. And, as we shall see, a common line of thought – originating in PowerGen – unifies this work. Underpinning it all, and responsible more than any other factor for its success is the care with which the foundations for each project are laid in the practice's own studio.

Rigour and respect

Three years ago, Bennetts Associates moved to premises in a small Clerkenwell side street. There, a small, three-story eighteenth century drovers' barn has been restored to form the hub of the new offices which include a larger mid-twentieth century printworks and the practice's own twenty-first century double-height infill workspace. The overriding impression is one of light, spaciousness and calm. The restrained use of colour and the clarity of the different forms of construction, ranging from the old brick and timber barn to the steel framed mezzanine and roof of the latest part, also catch the eye. Occupying the space is the majority of the 70-strong staff (14 are based in Edinburgh), of whom six are directors and one an associate director. Unusually, the male-female ratio of the architectural staff is 59:41, while overall (including administrative staff) it is 51:49 – a very high proportion of women.

At the core of the firm's architecture, regardless of building type, is a belief that it should serve its intended purpose and, at the heart of every Bennetts Associates project lies a highly developed brief. These are impressive documents. At Wessex Water, the brief ultimately exceeded 60 pages, whereas at the New Street Square office redevelopment it runs to a more typical 24 pages and includes an understanding of the client's general policies, strategic objectives for the proposed development and their position in the market. In other words, the architects confirm their understanding of the client's view of the world. Next there is, as one would expect from this practice, a long section on sustainability – economic, social and environmental: here, the needs of the capital city and the Holborn area are recognised. Requirements for element life spans and cost efficiency are followed by a lengthy section on office spaces: this ranges from atria environmental conditions to occupational patterns,

Bennetts Associates' Offices
Right: Brainstorming in the open plan space

PowerGen Headquarters
Right: Detail of atrium
space

Far right: View from the
car park, immediately
after completion

cores to column grids, and basement waterproofing to public art.
After a section on retail space, the brief concludes with another on
the public realm. In contrast, the brief for the Cummins engine plant
included everything from detailed descriptions of the production
processes to environmental conditions and the management themes
used by the company worldwide.

The design process, described more fully in Francis Duffy's
commentary, is normally linear, with design studies following the brief,
but there are, inevitably, circumstances when design ideas have to
be made evident before a brief is established. While diagrams are
being hand drawn, others in the team will be studying specific aspects
ranging from rights of light to townscape and functional relationships
to room counts, developing alternative plans and sections and
undertaking more complex, computer-based studies. The pivotal role
is that of the editor, selecting options and gradually honing these into
alternatives to be discussed with the client team. "The best moments",
says Rab Bennetts, "are the brainstorming sessions round the table,
when two or three people might actually be drawing on the same
sheet at the same time. And the best result is when it is the indivisible
product of a group, rather than of an individual." Members of the teams
are encouraged to challenge whatever ideas are on the table, whoever
the author.

Another director, Julian Lipscombe, sums up: "At the heart of
the practice is a strong moral and ethical core. 'Respect' is a key word
and covers a wide range of aspects, such as respect for colleagues
at all levels, respect for the particular needs of a client, respect for the
opinions and inputs of fellow consultants through to respect for

contractors and site operatives. Clearly also the respect for the planet
that has been important to the practice for nearly two decades is
related to this attitude. None of this is politically correct lip service but
has been in place since the inception of the practice. We believe that
the architect should be a strong leader but should not operate with
arrogance or ego. This requires him or her to be well rounded and
fully in command of the wide range of aspects involved in creating
architecture of the highest order."

The strong presence and memorable form of the completed
buildings (whether designed for end-users or for rental) is, then, the
result of rigorous analysis and respect for collaborators rather than a
search for an image and critical acclaim. Analytical rigour and respect
are, however, not enough to account for the consistently high standard
of architecture generated by this practice. It is therefore with the
identification of a common line of thought that this essay is primarily
concerned. The first clear statement of this can be found in the
PowerGen building.

A quantum leap in quality

Approached end-on, PowerGen lies along the contours of its gently
sloping site at the end of a Coventry business park. Its long, four-
storey, repetitively fenestrated brick-clad form has the scale and
simplicity of a nineteenth century mill building of the functional
tradition so admired by Rab and Denise. However, the huge car park
on the south side, the solar control louvres on the overlooking facade
and the carefully landscaped area to the north place it firmly in that
present which the quasi-domestic idiom of so many of its neighbours

seems to deny. Inside, the two halves of the long atrium have the scale and nobility of turbine halls — a reflection, perhaps, of the privatised company's origins in the former Central Electricity Generating Board. Thus, unlike most office buildings which are, too often, no more than the sum of their parts — the PowerGen headquarters offers a memory of a related building form, thus enabling the user to engage, however unconsciously, with the new building.

The building's dominant structure and clarity of organisation underpin a powerful sense of order. The circular concrete columns are, thanks to the glazed balustrades, visible for their full height and support a system of elegantly shaped vaults highly expressive of the forces contained within them. A separate, lighter, steel structure carries the atria roofs and makes a clear distinction between the spaces and their structures. The floor plans have a similar clarity. Office areas, unobstructed by cores and enclosed rooms, are accessed from a corridor along their inner edges. At each end and at the centre, three semi-enclosed staircases articulate the long top-lit central zone into two distinct spaces. The lifts are placed out of sight beyond the office security zone.

The lighting, both natural and artificial, is particularly striking. The atria and the outer edges of the office floors are naturally lit and the office areas themselves are illuminated by artificial light reflected from the vaults so effectively that there is no need for task lighting. Indeed, the lower edges of these brightly lit and beautifully shaped vaults transform the heavy structure into something of almost poetic beauty (curiously reminiscent of the podium understructure of Utzon's Sydney Opera House) a world away from the banalities of a suspended ceiling. Baffles prevent direct sunlight from penetrating into the atria but there is no such obstruction over the top-lit stairs where shafts of sunlight can be seen through the generously sized openings in the enclosure walls.

The use of materials is as unexpected as it is appropriate. Stack-bonded prefabricated brick panels reveal the cladding as subservient to the structure within the building. The superb quality of the in situ concrete vaults is a remarkable technical achievement giving an almost domestic finish to these formidable structural elements. In sharp contrast to the somewhat harsh glass and stainless steel aesthetic of so much corporate architecture, timber is used widely — and especially in places where people linger or on surfaces they touch. The principal circulation routes along the atria edges were floored in timber (now changed to laminate); a timber handrail tops the glazed balustrades; and, through the great sliding timber screens to the staircase towers, one catches a glimpse of the timber lining and stairs. These generously sized stair enclosures with their echoes of Louis Kahn (much admired by Bennetts Associates), have the luxurious feel of the inside of a giant cigar box and provide a pleasant place in which to encounter others.

Unsurprisingly, low energy use was a key client requirement. This large building is naturally ventilated and, with its opening windows, offers users a degree of control. Acoustically, too, this is a successful design — the elliptical section of the vaults eliminates the problems associated with perfectly arched vaults in offices elsewhere and the hum of activity at the base of the atria is in no way distracting. Users describe this as an enjoyable place to work in — one in which staff

tend to 'dress up' rather than 'down'.

One sense of the level of achievement represented by this building can be obtained by comparing it with, say, Arup Associates' much admired Gateway 2 building at Basingstoke, completed for Wiggins Teape twelve years earlier, in 1982 – for which Rab Bennetts was the project architect under Peter Foggo. The distance travelled has been immense. Gateway 2 was the first office building to employ an atrium as part of a natural ventilation system, drawing air through the surrounding offices and exhausting it at high level.[1] The atrium was really an extension of the reception area from which four separate exposed lift towers rose to connect with high level walkways. PowerGen resolves the relationship between atrium and office space and has an air of humanity that the earlier, rather mechanistic, building did not.[2] Both operationally and environmentally it is an undoubted success and now accommodates 300 persons more than the 600 it was originally designed for. And, from it, there has flowed a series of other office/atria buildings – such as John Menzies and BT Edinburgh Park – each with its own distinct *parti* and each equally successful.

Architecturally, there are certain characteristics clearly evident in the PowerGen building. It stakes out its territory and generates a strong sense of place; it seems in every way an appropriate solution to the brief; there is a powerful sense of order and clarity of circulation; the spatial gravitas of the interior is self-evident; daylight and natural ventilation bring the users closer to the natural environment; the use of materials and colour is sensual and sensitive to touch; and, inside, there is a sense of inclusivity and even enjoyment. Each of these

characteristics has been developed in the practice's subsequent work and, in the ensuing sections, we shall consider examples of their application.

Place making

PowerGen and its immediate successors were built on rural and suburban sites. At one extreme, the John Menzies and BT buildings on the Edinburgh Business Park are set within the context of Richard Meier's masterplan. At the other, Wessex Water settles unassertively onto a sloping site on the edge of stonewalled meadows at the end of a 40-kilometre long valley just outside Bath. Today, much of Bennetts Associates' work is urban and frequently involves masterplanning. Indeed, the practice may well have benefited from having worked on open sites before receiving commissions for urban buildings.

City Inn Westminster is one example of such an urban commission. Set on an unpromising site one block back from MI5's looming sub-Lutyens pile on Millbank, the new hotel (a type on which the practice had never before worked) has transformed the undistinguished backwater in which it is set. A new pedestrian route running along the edge of the site between John Islip Street, on which the hotel's entrance is located, and Thorney Street, where the service access is placed, has been created. This has increased the 'permeability' of the area, enabled the provision of a significant public artwork and greatly enhanced the public rooms within the hotel. Above the 'podium' containing the public and service accommodation, two towers set at an angle to each other skilfully accommodate the site's awkward geometries. These simple moves, combined with the elegant

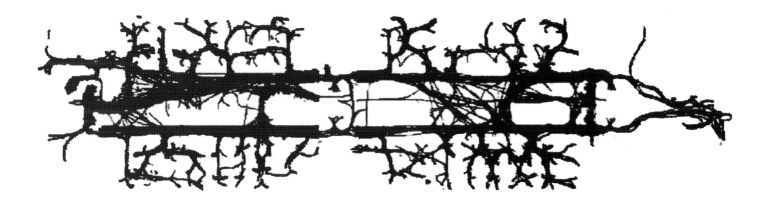

PowerGen Headquarters
Left: The in situ concrete vaults

Above: Ground floor connections, analysed by London University's Space Syntax unit

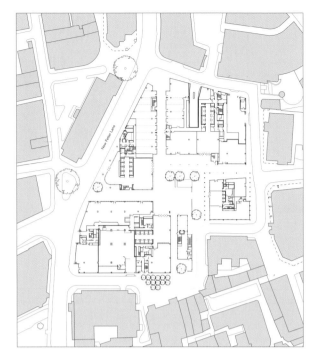

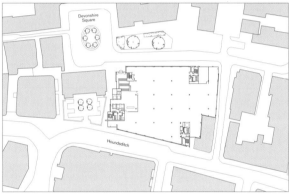

New Street Square
Above top: Site plan showing the building's relationship with its urban context

Devonshire Square Offices
Above: Site plan

and unostentatious architecture of the hotel itself have generated an air of quality which far exceeds that normally expected from an up-market budget hotel chain.

Closer to the City itself, in the Holborn area, the practice has been working in masterplanning mode on the redevelopment of New Street Square. Here, an unremarkable series of 1960s office buildings and a classic example of what the *Architectural Review* once described as 'sloap' (space left over after planning) is being replaced by a square around which are set two large floorplate and two conventional floorplate office buildings of varying heights with retail accommodation at ground level. Narrow pedestrian streets and an arcade link the new development back to the complex layout of the area surrounding the site. In developing and testing the urban layout, Bennetts Associates have worked closely with Space Syntax analysts from the London School of Economics' Cities Programme.[3] The architecture of the individual buildings is varied and deeply influenced by orientation but, linking the whole, is a common approach to city building and sustainability.

Both City Inn Westminster and New Street Square take possession of their respective sites in a gentle manner, exploiting their full potential but respecting the surroundings and providing the impetus for enhancement and regeneration. On a larger scale, at Brighton, the practice's newly completed, Labrouste inspired, library and square form the 'anchor' for the redevelopment of a run-down area of the North Laine. There, at night, seen through the great south-facing glazed screen, the library's beautifully lit and utterly astonishing reading room almost literally becomes part of the square and forms a modern, interior, counterpart to the floodlit exterior of Nash's exotic Royal Pavilion.

Appropriateness

While it is entirely appropriate for a Westminster hotel or a Brighton library to be distinctive buildings, it would surely lack decorum if every office building in the City of London strove to make its mark. (It is of course a sad fact – and a sign of the insecurity generated by the success of Canary Wharf – that so many of them do.) In this respect, Devonshire Square, the Royal Bank of Scotland's City offices, is a model for others.

This large building occupies most, but not all, of a block. Many of those who rush along the narrow, almost cavernous reaches of Houndsditch, must hardly notice it. This is not a street of any architectural or urban distinction – and the new building makes no attempt to draw attention to itself. In plan, the structural grid sits comfortably within the irregularly shaped site. At ground level, a large bar and a restaurant form extensions of the public realm, avoiding the pavement-level inhumanity of so many monofunctional City office buildings. But the most masterly stroke of all – the one that firmly ties this building into its context – is the location of the office entrance on the corner of Devonshire Square. From here, one is drawn into a lofty hall up a flight of stone steps set on the diagonal and gently rising to the reception desk at the foot of one of the building's two atria.

Above mezzanine level, the floor-to-ceiling glazing is set within an exposed dark grey-painted steel frame, more reminiscent of Chicago than the City. Through the glazing can be seen the silent drama of a major bank at work – a stark contrast to the invisible activities behind the almost impenetrable facades that surround it. Both vertically and horizontally, there is an air of inevitability in the way this large but modest building occupies its awkward site. Despite its speculative origin, it has a gritty presence and air of authority entirely appropriate to its site and its use by one of the nation's great banks. And, as with so many of the practice's buildings, this one is a pleasure to look at both during the day and after dark.

**Devonshire
Square Offices**
Above left: Facade
facing Houndsditch

New Street Square
Above right: Detail
of model

City Inn Westminster
Left: Massing model

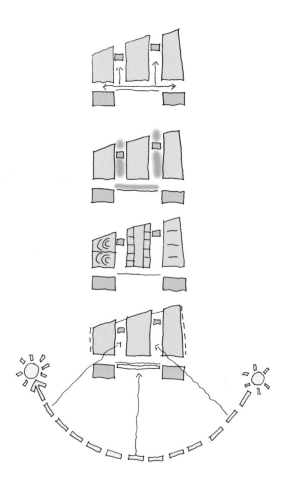

Cass Business School, City University
Above: Explanatory diagrams analysing (from top) circulation; light; usable space; sunpath

Above right: One of the two atrium spaces

Cummins Engine Company
Opposite: The assembly hall viewed from the administration offices

Such appropriateness of form, material and detail – and lack of ostentation – can be found in many other buildings by the practice. The emphasis ranges from an almost utilitarian directness at the Cummins assembly plant, to the joyfully fantastical setting of the Hampstead Theatre and the quietly noble ambience of the new Brighton Central Library (where the contractors attempted to persuade the architects to construct the wonderful sculptural form of the great concrete 'trees' in glass reinforced plastic).

Order and circulation

As so tellingly evident at PowerGen, the order in the practice's buildings derives primarily from the clarity and inter-relation of structure and circulation. Variations on the PowerGen theme are elegantly modulated in the Edinburgh offices of John Menzies and BT. At Wessex Water, a counterplay exists across the central 'street' between, on one side, the enclosing walls to the communal spaces and, on the other, the exposed steel structure of the offices where the central row of columns clearly positions the edge of the circulation spine.

At the City University's Cass Business School, the order derives not so much from the structure as from the organisation of the building into three parallel floor plates separated by two atria introducing daylight into the centre of a deep city block. The combination of quasi-solid volumes formed by stacking these floorplates and the long, deep voids between them enables the visitor to form an understanding of the layout of this densely occupied and complex building. An open staircase within the first atrium links the

entrance foyer and nearby cafe with the heavily used basement auditorium foyer and first floor learning resource centre. Elsewhere, on each floor, a wide corridor runs from the main block of lifts and stairs between, on one side, the light well to a ground level courtyard and, on the other, the ends of the atria, on each side of which routes run into the building. The lifts, as in virtually all the practice's buildings are discreetly concealed but the stairs here are glazed and fitted with a bench at each floor level so that chance encounters can develop into conversations. It is an infinitely more humane arrangement than the exposed lifts and concealed or 'feature' stairs of its neighbours.

Cass is an astonishingly complex building. It incorporates an extraordinary range of teaching, study, library, computer, dealing room, catering and office spaces. Open for 24 hours a day, it has to cope with the hourly 'tidal waves' of students entering and leaving lectures and seminars, with others making their randomly-timed visits to the library and study spaces, and with visitors and academic and research staff. It is surprisingly easy to 'navigate' – indeed, a sightless person would be able to find the way by simply detecting the differences between the carefully arranged noisier and quieter activities.

Spatial gravitas

Gravitas is not a word used by many architects – and certainly not in relation to offices and industrial plant. But it is part of Bennetts Associates' vocabulary and, as PowerGen proved, it is both achievable (at no extra cost) and beneficial in an office context. And not just in offices – for, together with the newly completed Brighton Central Library, the Cummins assembly plant at Manston in Kent represents,

rather improbably, one of the prime examples of this characteristic of the practice's work.

At Cummins, tall steel 'trees' support a beautifully articulated vaulted roof structure high above an almost square assembly area. One has to look hard to find the humans within this vast space and, in reality, it is the building and the larger diesel generators that dominate. The one touch of colour in the light grey interior is the 'safety-yellow' of the moving gantries and the units under assembly. The only sounds are of a component being hoisted, the brief whine of a power tool and the slightly muffled voices of a group discussing a production issue at one of the tables at the end of the assembly area nearest the offices. The noise of mechanically extracted air is absent – this is a naturally ventilated (and lit) building. At noon, on a fine, crisp, late autumn day, sunlight falls on the floor nearest the glazed screen and, deeper into the building, shafts of light slice across the deeply profiled 'tree trunks' while, above, the 45 degree geometry of the 'branches' is emphasised by the way they catch the light. This space is awe-inspiring. At night, artificially lit and seen from outside, the robustly noble structure has the air of an austere, elegantly crafted stage set. Cummins is famed for the quality of its buildings and the enlightened attitude of its management: it is hardly surprising that this is a place where people obviously enjoy coming to work.

The natural environment

Naturally ventilated and with an openable window within reach of each workplace, Wessex Water is, by all accounts, also good to work in. Offices on the lower floor of each wing have direct access to the

Gunnar Asplund
Left: Law courts extension to Göteborg Town Hall, 1937

Hampstead Threatre
Opposite: The cylindrical auditorium meets the rectangular foyer

landscaped courtyards while those above have splendid views. And, from the meeting rooms and restaurant, one can see over the fields and, on a fine day, right down the long valley towards Salisbury Plain. This is about as close to nature as you can get in a corporate headquarters.

So much for the working conditions. What about the building? Built on an old brownfield (hospital) site in an area of outstanding natural beauty, it is, despite its size, remarkably inconspicuous – indeed, it is hardly visible from the nearby road. Its stepped section hugs the slope and, seen from the fields below, the long lines of Bath stone parapets, finely detailed external sun-shading and grass covered roofs contrast sympathetically with the dry-stone walling and occasional trees in the surrounding fields. Within the two-level, partly sloping courtyards, the planting is generous but unfussy. And, below ground, tanks store the rainwater from the large expanse of metal-covered roofs for recycling in plant watering and toilet flushes.

As a privatised public utility company responsible for a natural 'product', Wessex Water places sustainability at the forefront of its operations. This building was required, in every respect, to be an example of this policy. In terms of energy efficiency, embodied energy, reduced transport emissions, waste reduction, waste water recycling and enhanced bio diversity it is indeed a model and, on completion in 2000, achieved the highest-ever BREEAM rating awarded to an office building.[4] Which goes to show that a traditional Modernist approach can result in buildings that perform every bit as well, if not better, than those adopting the clumsy gymnastics of 'sustainable architecture'.

Materials and colour
Some architects are famed for their obsession with materials, others for their use of colour. Bennetts Associates belong to neither category and yet each of their buildings demonstrates an inspired and appropriate use of both. Consider the great concrete vaults and the bright red meeting room enclosure at BT Edinburgh; the robust, exposed steel structure and coloured office end-walls at Wessex Water; and the great, grey steel frame and granite fin walls at Devonshire Square. In each of these, the combinations are almost sensual but never overdone.

It is not overdone at the Hampstead Theatre either – but it is very much more in evidence. The vast majority of the practice's buildings have light coloured timber handrails, supported on slender steel framing with glass balustrades set between. But here, at Hampstead, this simple arrangement is further developed. The handrails are in a rich dark American walnut extended to form a drink shelf around the foyer edges. Margins to the foyer floor, the bridge decks and stair treads are also formed in a dark hardwood. All this timber is a wonderful counterpoint to both the finely detailed exposed steel frame of the first floor offices and the curving zinc-sheeted carapace of the auditorium. But it is the form of the glazed balustrades that is unexpected. Here, instead of being partly framed, the glass sheets project forward from the uprights and above the handrail level. The resulting planar effect has a light, almost ephemeral quality which is all of a part with the festive atmosphere emphasised by the spotlighting, the billowing white canopies above the bar and the deep red colour of the wall behind it.

Timber is used in slatted form both outside the building, for the solar control screening, and, inside the auditorium, as a maintenance-free unifying surface that conceals acoustic adjustments. Colour is evident externally both in the deep blue of the blind end-walls and, at night, when Martin Richman's ever-changing light panels provide a background for the 'theatre of the street'. Internally, the same red of the bar wall is repeated in the auditorium seating and the rear walls of the stalls and circle. As a setting for public enjoyment and dramatic performance, this theatre could hardly be bettered.

Inclusivity and enjoyment
It was the Swedish architect, Gunnar Asplund, who coined the phrase "Forms that do not frighten but invite".[5] This description could well be applied to Bennetts Associates' work. The forms are unaggressive, the entrances clear. Although all these buildings contain the now inevitable security barriers, the entrance sequences are designed with such a generosity and lightness of touch that the visitor hardly notices them. At Brighton, the librarian, aware of the off-putting approach to so many older municipal libraries, comments on how pleased she is at the welcoming and generously sized entrance foyer. At each stage, the first-time visitor has plenty of time to map out the

Brighton Central Library
Right: Detail of library
skylight

Opposite: The mezzanine
floor viewed across the
lending library

route and any possible challenges along it.

In terms of inclusivity, much depends on the building user's policies and, in this respect, Bennetts Associates has been fortunate to work for many enlightened clients. At PowerGen there was a deliberate policy to break down the pre-privatisation staff segregation policies of the old Central Electricity Generating Board (CEGB); at Cummins, the enlightened employment policies of that company prevailed; at Wessex Water and Cass, the client developed a highly effective method of involving and informing staff throughout the briefing, design and construction phases; and, at Hampstead, the small scale and experimental nature of the theatre mean that audience and performers share the same entrance – there is no stage door.

But it is perhaps in the practice's ability to create appropriate settings for human activity that the source of its success in making buildings that are a pleasure to use lies. Of course, natural ventilation, good lighting and an awareness of the world outside contribute greatly to this – but so, too, does the awe-inspiring nature of the PowerGen atria; the quiet, daylit calm of the Cummins assembly floor; the lively, top-lit 'street' at Wessex Water with its glimpses of courtyard planting and distant fields; and so on, through many buildings, each with its particular characteristics, right up to the reading rooms below the graceful white 'trees' of the Brighton Central Library.

Buildings that work
Just as the photographs in architectural magazines are rarely populated, so, too, is the voice of the user rarely heard in architectural criticism. Setting out with the intention of 'enfranchising' this well-qualified group, it was almost disconcerting to discover almost nothing but positive comment.

One of the clients at PowerGen, Mike Coffey, now advises companies proposing to build new offices and often brings them to see the building. "This is an early 1990s building and we are still trying to replicate its conditions. It's still new to people. That's sad – the rest of the development industry should have moved on." Ray Sayer, who oversaw the construction of the Cummins plant and still works there is similarly enthusiastic, ten years on: "The natural light here impresses every one. The building has certainly aided production, will support future growth without expansion and was designed to protect asset value by being a flexible, re-usable space. With a 'good architecture does not have to cost a fortune' approach, it was an exercise in high specification, controlled cost and value for money packaging and designed to be a relatively low maintenance facility."

At Wessex Water, the building certainly works well, and when, at the opening, a journalist asked the chief executive what he would change, he replied "Nothing at all". Neil Fisher, who has worked in the building since completion says, "Everybody loves the building and, wherever you are in it, you have the advantage of seeing the landscape outside."

Anthony Clarke, the Hampstead Theatre's artistic director (effectively the chief executive) took over the building a year after its completion. He claims that "the building works in so far as the matters that matter to me are concerned – and acoustically, apart from an alleged Bermuda Triangle of about five seats, it is a treat". In the City, Clive Holtham, the academic most closely involved with

the design of the Cass Business School, is so enthusiastic that he even conducts workshops on it. While over in Westminster, the 'added value' of good design is proven by the increase of the planned room rate and the high occupancy levels in the City Inn. Finally, at Brighton, librarian Sally McMahon has no doubts: "We had a good understanding with Bennetts, between ourselves as end-users and them as architects – and that is most unusual. There's an amazing feeling of connection in this library – it's a most uplifting building."

Simon Harris, a property consultant who has worked closely with the practice ascribes its success largely to Rab Bennetts' habit of thinking about the spatial and structural issues simultaneously – and ahead of the engineers. He describes him as "brilliant and, thanks to his apprenticeship to Peter Foggo, able to think on several fronts at once. He is rigorous and straight forward, quietly assertive and completely unflashy – very good to work with." Conversations with clients confirm that the practice as a whole shares those values.

Innovation and delivery

This review has made little mention of Bennetts Associates' ambitious sustainability targets – in embodied energy, resource and energy use. Doing justice to this aspect of their work is simply impossible within the scope of this essay – but Richard Weston has mentioned the way in which single elements often become multi-functional. Floors act structurally, as air ducts taking advantage of thermal mass, as acoustic and light reflectors and as pre-finished ceiling surfaces. Likewise, elevations become complex, many-layered filters controlled both centrally and locally. Innovating simultaneously on as many fronts

as this – let alone on a single element – is highly unusual. It says much for the skill of the architects, the other consultants and the constructors that the results are so successful.

Another significant omission has been any mention of the ease and speed with which these innovatory buildings appear to be assembled. Just as the brief is very carefully and comprehensively prepared so, too, is the means of construction. Computer simulations are widely used and it is not unusual to see an assembly mock-up in the courtyard of Bennetts Associates' offices. Engineers' data, particularly on services, is rigorously cross-examined and the consultants state that it is unusual for architects to know enough about engineering to do this.

Moreover, of those mentioned, PowerGen, BT Edinburgh Park, Devonshire Square, City Inn, Brighton Central Library and the New Street Square development are all design-and-build projects – a procurement system which is not exactly associated with architectural quality. It is even more astonishing to learn that the Brighton Library is actually a PFI project.[6] The proponents of this system of procurement will no doubt wheel it out as an example of the quality possible within it. Bennetts Associates would, however, reject any such claim: in future, the practice is extremely unlikely to shoulder the economic consequences of creating a fine, workable and innovative building within the PFI system. But it speaks volumes for their determination and skill that they managed it.

**Wessex Water
Operations Centre**
Opposite: Detail of the
building seen against the
site's stone boundary wall

Buildings of significance

There is something rather improbable about some of Bennetts Associates' achievements. Making a success of a PFI project is one example but so, too, is the fact that the practice originally made its name through a series of innovative, successful and widely admired office buildings. Despite the huge importance of this building type, this is something that few other practices would even aspire to: commissions for public buildings of one kind and another are far more sought after. Bennetts Associates has revealed its skill there, too. Few building types are more critically appraised by their users than theatres and libraries, and both the Hampstead Theatre and the Brighton Central Library are greatly liked. And yet these and other highly successful buildings like the Cummins assembly plant, the Cass Business School and the City Inn Westminster are all first efforts: the practice had never before designed one of these types.

Equally improbable is the architectural discretion with which these buildings respond to the sustainability agenda. The athletic aesthetics of 'sustainable architecture' are entirely absent – these buildings do not parade their virtues. Seen across the fields from the west, one would never guess that Wessex Water was the sustainability success story of the late 1990s – the solar control louvres that cap the long, low elevation share a rare refinement with the tooled surface of the local stone parapets below them. Intriguingly, these same louvres reappear, for example, in the City Inn, in a purely architectural role – as a cornice or finishing piece at the top of a tall facade: they have little functional purpose other than some shading to the fully glazed top floor (and were first used in this way on the long north elevation at PowerGen). The practice's only overt use of one of the clichés of sustainable architecture, the wind tower, can be seen on the Brighton Library. Originally intended to be larger and formed in copper, these would have been a wonderfully witty twenty-first century play on the onion domes of the nearby Royal Pavilion. Casualties of the PFI process, their reduction in scale and transformation into powder-coated aluminium casings is much to be regretted.

Improbable, too – and especially in the office buildings – is the absence of any trace of a formula repeated again and again. Instead, we find specific solutions combined with continual development and performance improvements. Absent as well is that other characteristic of 'corporate architecture' – hi-tech's cold, mechanical sleight of hand with its excessive use of structural glazing, stainless steel tubing and polished stone. For Bennetts Associates' buildings do far more than advertise the organisations that occupy them. Their impact is more profound – they reflect the civilising values of these organisations and, in particular, their respect for staff and other users. Cummins and Wessex Water are obvious examples – but there are many others. Visible, too, is an unusual respect for the public realm. At one level, this is apparent in masterplanning and in a specific concern for the economic sustainability of a locality. At another, it is evident in the commitment to public art.

Underpinning all of this work is the practice's analytical approach, its willingness to set (with its consultants) high performance targets and its ability to innovate and deliver. Each of its buildings is the outcome of a particular, very clearly defined set of needs. The rigour and richness of the outcome is astonishing. Wessex Water has met all its sustainability and environmental performance targets and is an exquisitely beautiful building. Cummins combines operational efficiency with a degree of gravitas matched only by some of the heroic industrial buildings of the 1950s. The Cass Business School combines, in a highly legible and life-enhancing manner, an extraordinary range of functions on a downtown site for no more than comparable accommodation on far less restricted sites in Cambridge. And so on…

Complementing this analytical approach is an extraordinary level of competence in the art of construction. Whether at the scale of the great exposed steel structure at Devonshire Square, of the multi-functional ceilings at PowerGen, of the delicate solar control screens on the Wessex Water office wings or of the gallery balustrades at Hampstead, there is always a combination of invention, integration and good judgement. It is all the more astonishing that this has often been realised within the context of contemporary procurement methods that many architects find hostile to architectural and constructional quality. Indeed, architecture, construction and a commitment to effective delivery are inseparably united in the work of this practice. On the other hand, the deliberate search for architectural significance – or iconic status – is totally absent from this body of work. Despite this – and following a line of thought based on painstaking analysis, skillful synthesis and the inspired use of the traditional qualities of great architecture – Bennetts Associates continues to produce buildings of significance that respect the environment and place human needs foremost.

Notes

1 See Hawkes, D, "Air Apparent", in *The Architects' Journal*, 3 August 1983, pp26–34.
2 See Hannay, P, "Rooms with a View", in *The Architects' Journal*, 14 November 1984, pp55–66.
3 Earlier, the practice had worked on the internal planning of PowerGen with the Space Syntax Laboratory at University College London's Bartlett School of Architecture and Planning.
4 A BREEAM (Building Research Establishment Environmental Assessment Method) rating (ranging from 'pass' to 'excellent') identifies the level of the building's performance with respect to management, energy, health and safety, pollution, transport, land use, ecology and materials.
5 Quoted by Colin St John Wilson in "Gunnar Asplund and the Dilemma of Classicism", *Gunnar Asplund 1885-1940: The Dilemma of Classicism*, London: Architectural Association, 1988, p9.
6 PFI stands for Private Finance Initiative in which a company (usually formed by a consortia including a construction company, a bank and a facilities management company) will finance, construct and maintain a building for the public sector in return for an annual rent.

PROJECT DATA

Bennetts Associates' Offices, London, p26
Client Bennetts Associates
Architect Bennetts Associates with Baynes & Mitchell
Conservation adviser Richard Griffiths
Structural Engineer Price & Myers
Services Engineer Cundall Johnson & Partners
Cost Consultant Michael Latham Associates
Contractor Sames

BT Edinburgh Park, Edinburgh, p32
Client BT
Structural Engineer Blyth & Blyth Associates
Services Engineer Roberts & Partners
Landscape Architect Ian White Associates
Acoustic Consultant Sandy Brown Associates
Fire Engineer Jeremy Gardner Associates
Infrastructure Engineer Halcrow Waterman
Lighting Consultant Jonathan Speirs & Associates
Public Art Consultant Public Art Commissions and Exhibitions
Cost Consultant Tozer Capita
Project Manager Tozer Capita
Design-Build Contractor Balfour Beatty Construction Ltd

Cass Business School, City University, London, p36
Client City University
Structural Engineer Alan Baxter Associates
Services Engineer Whitby Bird & Partners
Landscape Consultant Abigail Concannon Associates
Acoustic Consultant Sandy Brown Associates
Lighting Consultant Speirs & Major
Fire Engineer Jeremy Gardner Associates
Cost Consultant Gardiner & Theobald
Planning Consultant King Sturge
Project Manager GTMS
Construction Manager Exterior International Ltd

Central Library and Jubilee Street Development, Brighton, p40
Client Brighton & Hove Councill/ Mill Group
Architect Bennetts Associates with Lomax Cassidy & Edwards
Structural Engineer SKM Anthony Hunt
Services Engineer Fulchrum Consulting
Landscape Architect Land Use Consultants
Acoustic Consultant WSP Acoustics
Fire Engineer Jeremy Gardner Associates
Sustainability Consultant BRE Centre for Sustainable Development
Access Consultant All Clear Designs
Design-Build Contractor Rok

Channel 4 Headquarters Competition, London, p46
Client Channel 4
Client Adviser Wheeler Consultancy Group
Structural Engineer Ove Arup
Services Engineer Ove Arup

City Inn Westminster, London, p48
Client City Inn Ltd
Structural Engineer Blyth & Blyth
Services Engineer Faber Maunsell
Interior Design (public areas) Proof Consulting
Art Consultant Modus Operandi
Cost Consultant Atkins Faithful & Gould
Design-Build Contractor Carillion

City Place Offices, Gatwick, p52
Client BAA Lynton (Developer), BT (Occupier)
Structural Engineer Buro Happold
Services Engineer WSP
Landscape Architect Hyland Edgar Driver
Cost Consultant Davis Langdon & Everest
Project Manager Buro Four Project Services
Contractor Bovis Lend Lease

City Road Basin, London, p56
Client London Borough of Islington and City Road Basin Limited (Masterplan), British Waterways, Miller Group and Groveworld (Residential)
Structural Engineer URS
Services Engineer SKM Anthony Hunt
Landscape Architect Whitelaw Turkington
Sustainability Consultant URS
Cost Consultant EC Harris

Cummins Engine Company, Kent, p58
Client Cummins Engine Co (Power Generation International)
Structural Engineer Whitby Bird and Partners
Services Engineer Ernest Griffiths & Son
Landscape Architect Roger Griffiths Associates
Fire Engineer Arup Fire
Cost Consultant Gardiner & Theobold
Project Manager Buro Four Project Services
Contractor Tarmac

Devonshire Square Offices, City of London, p64
Client BT Properties/Axa Sun Life Properties Ltd
Client Representative Ian David Ltd
Structural Engineer Whitby Bird/Waterman Partnership
Services Engineer Cundall Johnston and Partners
Fire Engineer Jeremy Gardner Associates
Cladding Consultant Arup Facade Engineering
Lighting Consultant Equation Lighting Design
Cost Consultant Davis Langdon & Everest
Planning Consultant Montagu Evans
Project Manager Buro Four Project Services
Design-Build Contractor Carillion Building Ltd

Exhibition Building Competition, Southern England 2003, p68
Client Confidential
Structural Engineer Buro Happold
Services Engineer Buro Happold
Landscape Architect Grant Associates
Sustainability consultant BRE
Cost Consultant Davis Langdon
Planning Consultant Montagu Evans

Guildford Civic Hall Competition, Surrey, p90
Client Taylor Woodrow Developments
User Guildford Borough Council
Structural and Services Engineer Buro Happold
Acoustic Consultant Arup Acoustics
Theatre Consultant Theatreplan
Cost Consultant Taylor Woodrow
Design-Build Contractor Taylor Woodrow

Hampstead Theatre, London, p92
Client Hampstead Theatre Foundation
Structural Engineer Curtins Consulting Engineers
Services Engineer Ernest Griffiths & Son
Acoustic Consultant Arup Acoustics
Theatre Consultant Theatreplan
Lighting Consultant Robert Bryan
Cost Consultant Citex Bucknall Austin
Project Manager Buro Four Project Services
Contractor Laing O'Rourke

Heathrow Airport Visitor Centre, London, p98
Client Heathrow Airport Ltd
Structural and Services Engineer Buro Happold
Landscape Architect Martin Popplewell Associates
Acoustic Consultant SRL
Exhibition Designer Media Projects International
Cost Consultant Philip Pank Partnership
Design-Build Contractor Shepherd Design and Build

Heathrow World Business Centre, London, p102
Client BAA (Lynton)
Structural Engineer WSP
Sunshading Engineer Adams Kara Taylor
Services Engineer Cundall Johnston & Partners
Landscape Architect Martin Popplewell Associates
Acoustic Consultant Ian H Flindell Associates
Public Art Consultant BAA
Cost Consultant Davis Langdon & Everest
Contractor Birse (Phase 1), LMK (Phase 2), MACE (Phase 3)

John Menzies Edinburgh Park, Edinburgh, p106
Client John Menzies (UK) Ltd
Structural Engineer Curtins Consulting Engineers
Services Engineer Blyth & Blyth
Landscape Architect Ian White Associates
Cost Consultant Banks Wood & Partners
Project Manager Buro Four Project Services
Management Contractor Bovis Construction Ltd

Loch Lomond Gateway and Orientation Centre, Dunbartonshire, p110
Client The Loch Lomond and the Trossachs National Park
Structural Engineer Buro Happold
Services Engineer Hulley & Kirkwood
Landscape Architect Ian White Associates
Exhibition Designer Campbell & Co Design
Public Art Consultant The Centre
Cost Consultant Banks Wood & Partners
Project Manager RM Neilson Partnership
Contractor Barry D Trentham

Medicentre, Inverness, p116
Client Inverness and Nairn Enterprise, Highlands and Islands Enterprise
Structural Engineer W A Fairhurst & Partners
Services Engineer K J Tait
Landscape Architect City Design Co-operative
Cost Consultant E C Harris LLP
Planning Consultant Turnberry Consulting
Contractor Tulloch Construction Ltd

Mark Lane Offices, City of London, p118
Client Hemingway Properties
Structural Engineer Whitby Bird & Partners
Services Engineer Cundall Johnson & Partners
Cost Consultant Davis Langdon & Everest
Planning Consultant Jones Lang LaSalle